THREE MEN ON THIRD

BOOKS BY IRA L. SMITH AND
H. ALLEN SMITH

THREE MEN ON THIRD

LOW AND INSIDE

THREE
MEN ON
THIRD

A BOOK OF BASEBALL ANECDOTES, ODDITIES, AND CURIOSITIES

H. ALLEN SMITH & IRA L. SMITH
WITH ILLUSTRATIONS BY LEO HERSHFIELD

BREAKAWAY BOOKS
HALCOTTSVILLE, NY
2000

Three Men on Third: A Book of Baseball Anecdotes, Oddities, and Curiosities

Copyright 1951 by H. Allen Smith and Ira L. Smith

ISBN: 1-891369-15-6

First paperback edition, April 2000

Published by BREAKAWAY BOOKS
P.O. Box 24
Halcottsville, NY 12438
(800) 548-4348
www.breakawaybooks.com

For a list of other sports literature titles published by Breakaway Books, see the last
two pages of this book, or, for more details, visit our website.

FIRST PAPERBACK EDITION

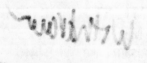

THREE MEN ON THIRD

PREFACE

THIS IS a companion volume to a book of baseball anecdotes and oddities which was published in the spring of 1949 under the title *Low and Inside*. That earlier book, which had a surprisingly large sale, was restricted to baseball incidents occurring prior to World War I; no such limitation obtains in the present volume.

The history of baseball is made up of forty per cent statistics and sixty per cent anecdote. It may be that a few nontoxic statistics have crept into our pages, although our aim has been to entertain rather than to manipulate decimal points; this book was written on a typewriter, not a comptometer. Your real devout baseball fan is a worshiper of statistics. He cares little for the so-called human interest side of the game. He is not amused by the fact that Elmer Popple, the outfielder, has six toes on each foot. What interests him is that Elmer Popple has a batting average of .324, hit 27 home runs, batted in 143 runs, hit for a total of 303 bases, weighs 183½ pounds, and measures 9¾ inches from ear lobe to ear lobe. The spectacle of three men on third does not amuse him. Quite to the contrary, he is enraged by such a spectacle, for he is a baseball purist. We, the authors of this book, are chiefly interested in a single statistic when we consider Elmer Popple: the twelve toes he carries around in his shoes. And we are greatly amused by the three men on third.

Out of the 1950 baseball season came a situation which exemplifies this difference in attitudes. That was the season in which Dizzy Dean was brought up to the big time as a television commentator for the New York Yankees. Within a week after he had started his new job the statistical purists were complaining. They got no amusement whatever out of Dizzy's unorthodox performance at the microphone. They were furious when, on occasion, Diz would suddenly forget the ball game altogether and break into song about goin' fishin' in th' craw-dad hole. To the statistical fan baseball is a dead-serious business. There's no room in it for frivolity. If a cat comes scampering onto the playing field and eludes capture for ten minutes, holding up the progress of the game, they are indignant about it, and cuss the cat and cuss the rest of us who whoop and cheer.

Dizzy Dean represented, then, a new and delightful diversion to us; the things he did and the things he said were often as entertaining as the ball games he was describing, or neglecting to describe. Much of the stuff that has been written about him since his assignment with the Yankees has missed the mark. Even as astute a writer as Joe Williams insists that Dizzy says "slud" for "slid." Never. What he says is "slood," making it rhyme with wood. Someone else, trying to write an account of Dizzy's appearance on a television panel show, also missed the boat. Dizzy was seated next to H. V. Kaltenborn during that program, and Mr. Kaltenborn needled him gently about his abuse of the English language, whereupon Diz responded: "Well now, I tell ya, Mr. Kattlinbomb, it's this way . . ."

There are, of course, many do-gooders who would like to see Dizzy barred from channels of public communication on the grounds that he is exercising a deleterious influence on the hordes of children who listen to his Ozarkian rhetoric. These complainants say that if it isn't stopped, the children will inevitably begin talking the way Dizzy talks. Well, suppose they do. It's talkin', ain't it?

Dizzy has certain locutions which recur frequently in his haphazard narration of a ball game. A player threw a ball, or thode it. An umpire is an umparr. Everybody on the playing field does everything nonchalantly. That is one of his favorite words. "There he goes," says Diz, "walkin' nonchalantly up to the plate." He spoke once of a passed batter "trottin' nonchalantly down to first." And of another as "squattin' nonchalantly in the on-deck circle." Once when a batter had fanned, Dizzy described him as "walkin' nonchalantly back to the dugout in diss-gust." The TV screen one day was holding a close-up of home plate while Catcher Yogi Berra was out at the mound conferring with his pitcher. As Berra started back to his position his feet and then his legs came into view at the top of the television screen. Said Diz: "There comes Berra's shin guards walkin' nonchalantly back to the plate." And again, "That tremenjous roar you hear is Ted Williams walkin' nonchalantly up to the batter's box."

Sometimes a batter "walks disgustilly" to the dugout after fanning. Sometimes he "stands confidentially" at the plate. And the players come off the "bainch" to "take their respectable positions."

A ball is "farred over to second" and a third strike sometimes "retarrs the side." When a pitcher fields a bunt Diz says: "He bounced on it like a cat on a mouse." A hard-hit ground ball that gets away from an infielder is usually described as having "karmed off his glove."

Dizzy speaks of "sprang training" and "peench hitters" and

the relief hurler "throwin' down his plimminary pitches." He summarizes, "No hits, no runs, and no airs." Errors are always airs. He describes conferences "in the middle of the diament." He says time has been called while a base runner "is lacening up his shoes." He becomes the baseball expert when he remarks, "They's gonna be a little fancy stragedy pulled now." The adverb "far" is always "for" in the Dean lexicon. "Lopat's got five strike-outs in the ball game so for," he says. Or, "As you seen on your screen, that's the first air of the ball game so for." He describes a hard-laboring pitcher as having "pussperation clean thew his uniform." And in announcing a pamphlet which the public may get by writing in, he says, "You can have the new Yankee sketch book if you woosh."

During a close shot of a batter, Dizzy advises: "Look careful now and you can see the heesive tape on his neck." Once when Joe DiMaggio made a magnificent catch deep in center—running with his back toward the plate and reaching high above his head to snag a fly ball, Dizzy yelled: "Holy cow! He caught it with his back in front of the pitcher's box!"

In a pre-season exhibition game at the stadium Dizzy uttered the following remarkable sentence: "That loads the Brooklyn Dodgers fulla bases." Speaking once of a player coming up to bat, he said, "He resembles Crosetti like he used to look." And on the occasion of a spirited rhubarb, he remarked: "They better watch out. That umparr used to be an ex-fighter." He is usually contrite when he makes a mistake in' calling a play. "I *bag* your pardon!" he says.

"This is what you call a real slugger's fest," he explained one day. And for the benefit of the amateur scorekeepers: "You gotta give the pitcher a sist on that." Discussing Ted Williams admiringly, he said: "Look at that stance on him! Brother, they's rhythm in that stance!" And of the Red Sox catcher: "Most all ballplayers got nicknames and Birdie Tebbetts's is Birdie because he's always a-hollerin' like a little ole kinairy

12

bird." Recalling the career of Dolph Camilli he said: "There was one of the gracefulest first basemans I ever seen." And during a tight situation in a close game, he remarked, "Brother, they's a lotta nerve-wrackin' out there on that field right now." Dizzy's comment on the lazily relaxed manner of Joe Gordon was: "Look at 'im. There's a fella you look at 'im you say, there's a fella dreads to do *anything*."

Sometimes Dizzy tries to be helpful to his audience, explaining things about baseball itself or about his own manner of speech. He spoke once of the futility of quarreling with an umpire, saying, "You might as well try to argy with a stump." After a moment's reflection, he continued: "Some of you New York folks might not know what a stump is. Well, I'll tell ya. A stump is a wood thing . . . well, it's somethin' a tree has been cut down off of."

One day when a visiting manager was making his way to the mound for the purpose of yanking his pitcher, Dizzy filled in with information out of his own vast experience.

"You folks," he said, "prob'ly wonder what's goin' on out there—what they're sayin' to one another. Well, I had some experience pitchin' and I can tell you what's goin' on. In the first place, that pitcher he's hot as a farrcracker. And he prob'ly don't like the idee of bein' took out. So when the manager comes walkin' nonchalantly out to the mound, the pitcher he says, 'Aw, fer cryin' out loud!' So the manager he says, 'Now take it easy, son. You cain't win *ever* day.' So the pitcher he says, 'Aw, fer cryin' out loud! If I coulda got that one guy out, that bum, they never woulda got nowheres offa me.' Then the manager he says, 'Now take it easy, son. You go on and take a sharr and git some rest and maybe you can beat 'em tuhmarr.' So the pitcher's purty burned up, and he says, 'Aw, fer cryin' out loud!' But he's gotta go, so he goes. That's approxi-mate-ly what goes on out there at the mound, folks."

At times he becomes a philosopher, as in his salute to Phil

Rizzuto when the Yankee shortstop insisted on staying in the game after being hurt. "Brother," exclaimed Diz, "I wanna tell you that's determination and will parr to play baseball!"

One day at stretch time in the seventh, he remarked, "Well, the fans has all stood up and woosht the Yankees good luck."

Approaching the plate, a batter once bent over to get some dirt on his hands, eliciting from Dizzy the following observation: "I want you folks to take a good look at that. Lookit him rubbin' his hands around in the dirt. I 'member when I was a little kid and useta go out and play in the dirt and then when we'd go home our mothers would whip us. Well sir, right there in fronta your eyes is big grown men out there playin' in the dirt. Dog-gone if this ain't a crazy world!"

The camera, which Dizzy always calls the camery, moved up close to an umpire standing near second base one afternoon.

"Lookit that umparr," said Diz, "standin' out there with his arms behind his back. Umparrs don't never seem to know what to do with their hands. They either got them behind their backs or folded. Lookit 'im out there! Looks sorta like a statcha."

Dizzy complains frequently about the amount of written material that is handed him in the course of a game because he has to read it and he doesn't like to read. After struggling through a long commercial one afternoon he concluded with: "Well, at least I got through to the end. I admit I cain't read good. But they's one thing I know. When that pitcher thows that ball, he thows it. When that ketcher ketches it, he ketches it. And when that hitter hits it, he hits it. That's all you gotta know, folks."

Television, as everyone knows, has enlarged the public interest in baseball to a phenomenal degree. It comes pretty close to being the chief topic of conversation among all classes of American people nowadays, being talked about more frequently than sex or the weather. One of the authors of this book en-

14

joyed an experience not long ago which illustrates the power the game holds over some of our citizens. In the summer of 1949 he was en route to California by train and arrived in Chicago on a hot Sunday morning, with several hours to wait before departure of his California train. Seeking some means of passing the time (he had already prayed extensively for the human race, so there was no occasion to go to church), he approached a taxi driver outside the railroad station.

"I've got some time to waste," he explained, "and in all this heat, maybe it would be a good idea to take a long ride. How about driving me along the lake front for a while?"

"I getcha," said the driver.

As the cab started toward the lake, the passenger said:

"Look, I'm a sort of stranger in Chicago. Know very little about the town. So, while you're driving along, if we pass anything that's interesting, point it out to me. You know what I mean?"

"I getcha," said the driver. He proceeded to Michigan Boulevard and the lake front and started north. The cab passed all manner of interesting-looking buildings and bridges and hotels and monuments and shore installations, but never a word from the driver. On and on he drove, saying nothing, apparently believing that he was passing no institution worthy of mention. At last—it seemed at least a half hour had elapsed—he suddenly whipped over to the curb.

"Now," he said, "lean over and look out the winda, over to the right there. See that big place? Well, sir, you're lookin' at the hotel where that broad shot Eddie Waitkus."

The title of this volume doesn't signify that the book's contents are concerned with the old Brooklyn Dodgers, who were sometimes called the Daffiness Boys. The predicament of having three base runners ganged up on third is associated with the Dodgers, though it is not an attainment that belongs to them exclusively. The day that Brooklyn accumulated three runners on third was August 15, 1926, when the Dodgers were engaging the Braves at Ebbets Field. In case you don't remember it, here are the details:

Brooklyn came to bat in the seventh. Johnny Butler singled. DeBerry hit a two-bagger, scoring Butler. Dazzy Vance singled and DeBerry went to third. Fewster was hit by the pitcher, filling the bases. Jacobson popped out. Babe Herman now took his place at the plate. The stage was all set for the drama. Herman belted a line drive to right field and DeBerry vacated third base and crossed the plate. Vance, who had been on second, thought Herman's drive was going to be caught, and held up until he was certain the outfielder had missed it; then Dazzy started for home. He rounded third, ran halfway to the plate, decided he wouldn't be able to beat the throw-in, reversed himself and started back to third. Meanwhile Fewster was tearing around the base paths from first, arriving at the third sack about the time Vance returned to it. They stood and looked at each other in astonishment for a few moments and then switched their attention to an even more astonishing sight. Babe Herman figured he had a double, possibly a triple, and he preferred a triple of course, and was bent upon trying to stretch it. He had his head down and was running for all he was worth, with no suspicion in his mind that a traffic jam had already developed at third. He didn't raise his head until he was a few feet from third and then when he looked up, there stood Vance and Fewster, and the Boston third baseman was just taking the throw. This third baseman, Taylor, was understandably excited. He received the throw and started tagging people. He tagged every human within reach, including the third-base umpire. Herman, however, had got himself out of range and was heading back for second. Taylor fired the ball down to the shortstop, and Herman was tagged out before he could reach the bag.

That episode became a sort of baseball classic, possibly because the unpredictable Babe Herman was involved in the making of it. Bennett Cerf has told the story of the time, a few years later, when Quentin Reynolds was sitting in the last row of seats in the grandstand at Ebbets Field during the early innings of an important game. Chancing to look into the street outside the park, Reynolds saw a late-comer, a Brooklyn fan who was running along the pavement, puffing heavily as he headed for the entrance.

"Better hurry up!" Reynolds yelled down to the man. "You're missing something big. The Dodgers have three men on base."

"Yehr?" cried the fan. "Which base?"

Other teams have put three men on third, or come pretty close to it. The impeccable Yankees of the early 1930s got so peccable one day in a game with Washington that they came within inches of achieving it. Washington was ahead 6 to 4 and the Yankees were batting in the last of the ninth. Lou Gehrig was on second and Dixie Walker was on first with Tony Lazzeri at bat. Tony hit the first pitch far over Goslin's head in right center field and the fans in the stadium went wild. It looked like a cinch for two runs.

As it had happened to Dazzy Vance, Gehrig on second thought that Goslin was going to catch the ball and was late getting started for home. Dixie Walker, however, was in a better position to see the ball, realized that it was uncatchable, and was off to a fast start.

By the time Gehrig rounded third Walker was right at his heels. There was a momentary hesitation on the part of the two runners, because the ball, retrieved by Goslin, was on its way in to the plate. Both Gehrig and Walker, however, noted that Tony Lazzeri was steaming past second and headed for third. Perhaps the thought flashed through their minds that a horrible and disgraceful situation was brewing—that they were about to get three men on third the way it had happened in

Brooklyn, and they simply couldn't let such a thing occur to the vaunted Yankees. In any event, Gehrig and Walker now turned on the steam and started for home. As they came down the third-base line, Walker looked as if he was about to run right up Gehrig's spine—they were that close. At the plate stood Luke Sewell, Washington's catcher, a nice fat baseball in his hand. He just stood there, like a statcha, and as the Yankee tandem arrived, ploppity-plop, he tagged them out and the victory belonged to the Senators.

MANY YEARS AGO an umpire named Morgan was associated with the Western League. This Morgan was a man who had implicit faith in the fair-mindedness and sportsmanship of the average baseball fan. He wasn't to keep that faith.

He was umpiring behind the pitcher in a game between Denver and Sioux City. He had made a whole series of decisions on close plays in favor of the visitors, Sioux City, and the Denver fans were howling at him and throwing an occasional bottle in his direction. Finally he called a third strike on another Denver player and now the abuse came down upon him in a torrent. In the crowd was one man who apparently had been brought up in poolrooms, for he put together a combination of shameful words, screaming them at Umpire Morgan with all the lung power at his command. It was an insult to end all insults, involving terminology out of dogdom, birth out of wedlock, and allegations of irregularities in the art of love.

Umpire Morgan called time. He stepped toward the grandstand, raising his hands to command quiet. Then he spoke:

"Ladies and gentlemen," he said, "I heard that remark. I consider the man who shouted it to be a coward. He doesn't have the courage to stand up and admit that he spoke those words. If he *does* have the courage, let him stand up now."

Every man in the crowd stood up.

ONE MORNING in 1941 readers of a certain Chicago newspaper found an exceptionally fine action picture staring out at them from the sports page. It was a close shot of a White Sox player sliding into third base. There was considerably more behind the picture than just that.

In the first place the runner in the picture had stolen third— a rare sort of thing in these days of powerhouse baseball. He had stolen third, moreover, at a time when he shouldn't have been up to any such shenanigans. He had been on second, with nobody out, and the steal was uncalled for, theoretically.

When the actual play occurred, Manager Jimmy Dykes was thoroughly shocked at what he was seeing. He popped out of the dugout and yelled at Mule Haas, the White Sox coach at third: "What in the name of God is going on down there? You outa your mind?"

Haas, who obviously had hung out the steal sign, seemed unperturbed. As Manager Dykes came charging out to get an explanation, Haas was ready with one.

"This fella here," he said, indicating a press photographer standing a few feet away, "came up to me and says he wanted to get a good action picture, like a man sliding into third, so I just tried to help him out."

Dykes swayed slightly on his feet, in the manner of a man bereft of his faculties, and then tottered back to the bench, speechless.

It was a real good news picture.

SOME OF THE gamiest baseball games in history were played in the Kentucky-Indiana-Tennessee League during the season of 1936. They smelt. In May of that year the Paducah club was struggling for leadership in the league. The team was on the road, playing Mayfield, and there was a hitch in the routine by which the club uniforms were given a pre-game cleaning. The Paducahs faced the Mayfields one afternoon in uniforms that were only slightly soiled. It seemed that the visitors could do no wrong that day, and they walloped Mayfield 13 to 4.

In the dressing room a player approached Ben Tincup, the Paducah manager, and said:

"I ain't superstitious—never was—but seems like to me it was these dirty uniforms made us do so good out there today. Why don't we jest go on playin' with 'em dirty, see what happens."

"Well," said Ben Tincup, "I want you to understand that I ain't a bit superstitious, but maybe you got something. Suppose we try it."

So they tried it. They resolved that they would not have their uniforms cleaned until they had won the championship for the first half of the season. By mid-July they looked as though they had been sleeping in their uniforms, in coalbins. It was said that they were able to steal bases almost at will for the reason that opposing infielders refused to hold them close to the bags. It was said that opposing catchers couldn't see too well through the fetid fog that hovered around the plate when Paducahs were at bat. One thing is certain—Paducah never once dropped out of first place in the standings during the period in which they played dirty.

SEVERAL YEARS AGO the newspapers reported that either a play or a movie was being written around a somewhat remarkable situation—the hiring of a girl pitcher by the Brooklyn Dodgers. Deponents knoweth nothing about whatever happened to the project, but deponents knoweth that the idea was not as farfetched as it sounds.

During the 1930s when the fabulous Joe Engel was boss of the Chattanooga club, the local fans never knew what to expect next from him. One day when the New York Yankees came in for an exhibition game, Engel suddenly startled the whole baseball world by sending in a girl pitcher, and be-dogged if she didn't fan both Babe Ruth and Lou Gehrig.

There is even an instance in which a girl took a turn at bat in a regular major-league game. The Cardinals were playing at Cincinnati on the last day of July in 1935. Thirty thousand spectators were jammed into a park with seating facilities for twenty-four thousand. The crowd overflowed onto the field and there was much confusion. Halfway through the contest the game had to be halted for fifteen minutes while the cops herded the fans back from the foul lines. During the last four innings the spectators were jammed so close to home plate that the batters had difficulty shouldering their way up to the plate.

Among the rabid fans in the mob near the plate was Miss Kitty Burke. At the beginning of the eighth inning Miss Burke engaged in some banter with Joe Medwick as he waited for his turn at bat. She spoke disparagingly of Medwick's abilities as a hitter, and remarked with some feeling that she, Kitty Burke, could out-hit him any day in the week.

The first half of the eighth ended and it was Cincinnati's turn to bat, with Herman first up. Miss Burke was still thinking about her conversation with Medwick when Herman came through the crowd. Suddenly she reached out, grabbed the bat out of his hands, walked to the plate and faced the pitcher.

Paul Dean was on the mound for the Cardinals and if he was shocked by the sudden appearance of a female in the batter's box, he showed little evidence of it. He simply wound up and lobbed a soft one down to her. Kitty took a good cut at it for a gal, and got the wood on it, but it was a dribbler, rolling back to the pitcher. Dean snatched the ball off the turf, looked up and saw Miss Burke loping hard toward first base. He

started to throw her out, then thought better of it. He concluded that the thing had gone far enough. So Miss Kitty Burke ran out her single and then, on the advice of the umpires, yanked herself from the game.

"Well," said Paul Dean afterward, "I guess that gives me a record. I'm the only big-league pitcher that a dame ever got a hit off uv."

JUDGE EDWARD T. DIXON of the Common Pleas Court in Cincinnati had a vexatious problem during the baseball season back in 1920. Judge Dixon's young son had a burning desire to see Babe Ruth hit a home run. The boy, living in a National League city, was genuinely unhappy and promised to remain in that state until he got to see the Babe pickle one.

Early in August Judge Dixon sat down to plan his vacation, and of course he thought of the boy's yearning, and called him in and said:

"Tell you what we're going to do. We're going on a Babe Ruth vacation. I've looked up the schedule and the Yankees open a series in Cleveland day after tomorrow. We'll go to Cleveland."

Father and son were in the stands, then, at Cleveland. In the first game of the series the Babe went hitless. In the second game he twisted his ankle and had to be carried off the field. The judge was more interested in the seriousness of that injury than the Yankee management.

The Yankees moved on to Washington. Judge Dixon and son came in right behind them, hoping. The Babe was still *hors de combat,* but there was a chance he might get back into action. He did—in the second game of the Washington series and, in beautiful fact, hit a long home run over the right-field fence.

That night Judge Dixon and his contented son were on a train headed back for Cincinnati, and the judge, a little weary, was quietly thinking about plans for his next vacation. He'd go fishing.

IN THE TIME when Lou Gehrig was at the peak of his magnificent career, the Yankees found themselves one afternoon playing an exhibition game with a minor-league team in a certain southern town. The kid pitcher for the bush-league team was showing surprising ability against the powerful Yanks and had gone through five innings without getting mauled.

Gehrig came to bat in the sixth and the young pitcher stared down at him for a long time before going into his windup. Then he threw one in the groove—a fast one that came right down the middle. Gehrig hit it and knocked it three blocks.

When the pitcher returned to the bench at the end of the inning his manager was waiting with a large question. "Why on earth," he demanded, "did you give him that fat one? You worked on him good before, and got him. What ailed you?"

"Well," said the young man, "it's like this. I know I'm not enough of a pitcher to ever get into the big leagues, and anyway, it won't be long till I've got to quit baseball and take over my dad's grocery business. And when I get back home I won't ever get a chance to see the big fellas in action. So when Gehrig came up to the plate, I got to thinking about it, and how I always wanted to see Lou hit one over the fence, the way him and the Babe do it, so I laid one in there for him. Now I can say I seen him do it."

24

A FRIVOLOUS SEA GULL appeared over the ball park at St. Augustine, Florida, one afternoon in 1946 when a Florida State League game was in progress. It seems unlikely that the bird knew that the ball game was a ball game; it is highly improbable that the critter was interested in the score. Yet that sea gull behaved almost like a Yankee fan. It swooped back and forth, flying low, staying always near the infield. The players went on with the game, somewhat nervously, and several times line drives narrowly missed the bird.

Finally the umpires called a recess. It had become apparent to them that the ball *might* hit that damn bird, and then what? They held a conference and concluded there ought to be a ground rule covering the matter. They made one. If a batted ball struck a sea gull, they announced, the batter would be entitled to a ground-rule double. Having so ruled, the contest was resumed, and immediately, just as if he had overheard the conference, the sea gull aimed himself toward the ocean and took his departure.

DAN WINSTON, a citizen of Gotham, poked his tongue into his cheek one day in 1939 and wrote a letter to the sports editor of the New York *Times*. This is what he had to say:

"Baseball being a strictly mercenary game at best, I have been wondering what has kept the magnates from seizing upon a simple yet logical means of adding to their purses.

"The plan, though it may sound silly, is as sensible as the placing of advertisements around the walls of the ball parks. Simply sell space on the players' uniforms.

"The potentialities of the idea are unlimited. Players would be classified according to known foibles, habits, or whims. For any outstanding physical feature an advertiser undoubtedly would pay an extra royalty."

Mr. Winston's letter suggests a little game in which individual players are matched with products they might advertise on their shirts. Some samples:

> Joe DiMaggio—spaghetti sauce.
> Bobby Thomson—Scotch tape.
> Harry Brecheen—cat rations.
> Allie Reynolds—Navajo blankets.
> Harry Walker—hats.
> Leo Durocher—motion pictures starring Laraine Day.

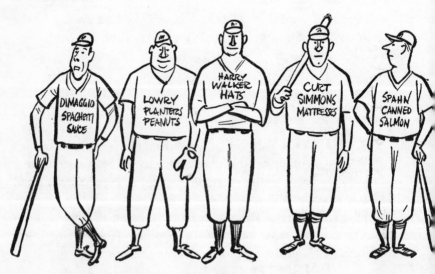

Harry Lowrey—Planters Peanuts.
Marty Marion—canned octopus meat.
Stan Musial—a book, The Cardinal.
Bill (Swish) Nicholson—mouth wash.
Phil Rizzuto—motor scooters.
Hank Sauer—kraut.
Enos Slaughter—country-cured hams.
Ted Williams—a lady's chemise, or shift.
Ewell Blackwell—riding crops.
Willie Jones—plum puddin'.
Bob Lemon—meringue pie.
Hal Newhouser—prefabricated dwellings.
Curt Simmons—mattresses.
Warren Spahn—canned salmon.
You take it from there. Or leave it lay, if you
    prefer.

THE WINSTON PLAN for advertising on baseball uniforms may have inspired an umpire who officiated at an exhibition game between the Dodgers and the White Sox at Cooperstown in 1943. Painted on the umpire's chest protector, in large and brilliant letters, was an advertisement for a Cooperstown taxicab service. And the Cooperstown stunt, reported in the press, may in turn have inspired Mr. Edward Hinko of Utica, N.Y., who did a lot of umpiring around his home town.

About a week after the Cooperstown game Hinko got a call from the president of the Eastern League asking him to fill in for a regular umpire who was sick. Hinko's first assignment was to team with Umpire George MacDonald, one of the league's veteran officials, in a double-header between Utica and Hartford. MacDonald worked behind the plate in the first game, and then it was Hinko's turn.

When Umpire MacDonald had taken his place near first, he glanced down toward the plate and got a shock. There stood Hinko, wearing a chest protector on which was blazoned a taxicab ad. MacDonald called for time and hurried down for a conference with his colleague. "That sort of thing," he said, indicating the ad, "is beneath the dignity of an Eastern League umpire. I think you'd better turn it around and hide the ad."

Hinko complied and there, on the reverse side of the protector, was an even more glaring ad—this one for a certain brand of drinking whisky.

"Gad," cried MacDonald, "zooks! Turn it back to the taxicabs! There's not a pitcher in the league who wouldn't blow sky high if he had to work with a liquor ad staring him in the face!"

Thus were taxicabs advertised in Utica.

A CHARACTER called "Hatpin Mary" arose to fair prominence around the wrestling arenas of New York, largely through the instrumentality of Dennis James, the television sportscaster. This lovely lady acquired her nickname from the fact that she sometimes climbed halfway into the ring and, using a hatpin, stabbed a wrestler she hated.

There was a time, long ago, when it wouldn't have been strange if the sporting-goods stores had started stocking hatpins as articles of standard athletic equipment. They were used quite extensively in baseball.

The two most prominent hatpin strategists were Harry O'Hagen and Red Andreas.

O'Hagen developed his technique when he was first baseman for Waterbury in the Connecticut State League. For quite a period O'Hagen had a record of catching more runners off first base than was reasonable. He had a hatpin fastened in his glove, with the point protruding at one side. By flicking a finger he was able to draw the point back into concealment an instant after it had done its work. The pitcher would throw to first. The base runner would dive or slide back to the bag. As his foot or hand made contact with the base, O'Hagen would flick him with the glove, giving him a light stab. The foot or the hand would recoil, naturally, away from the bag, and O'Hagen would quickly slap the ball on the runner for an out. He got away with it for a surprising length of time and then the officials caught on and ordered him to desist, under pain of getting his block knocked off.

Red Andreas was manager of the Sioux City team many years ago, and among the problems he had to face, whenever he took his team to Denver, was the rude behavior of the Denver third baseman, named Lee "Bird Dog" Quillen. (Quillen was called "Bird Dog" for the reason that one day on a hunting trip he had shot his own dog, mistaking it for a partridge.) Quillen had developed a technique of giving the hip to base runners as they rounded third, throwing them off stride and slowing them down in their progress toward home plate. Red Andreas decided to fight fire with fire.

During fielding practice Andreas concealed a hatpin beneath second base. He then told his players what he had done, and gave them their instructions. When one of them arrived on second, he was to call time and pretend to tie a shoelace; actually he was to snaffle the hatpin from under the bag. After that if the runner got a chance to try for home, he was to have the hatpin ready as he rounded third and when Bird Dog Quillen tried to bump him, he was to jab that hatpin into the third baseman's hind end—up to the hilt if need be. All during one game Bird Dog Quillen was subjected to the indignity of the hatpin. In the end he decided he would use his hips in the future only for sitting down.

MANY YEARS AGO a game between the Philadelphia Athletics and the Washington Senators turned into a free-for-all fight—one of the wildest battles ever seen on an American League diamond. At that time there was considerable in the way of ill feeling between the two clubs, and the gang fight started after a player had been spiked at the plate.

Almost everybody in uniform was in there swinging, but there was at least one player who didn't choose to get into the scrap. He was Big Joe Krakauskas, a Washington pitcher. Big

Joe was famous for his wildness as a pitcher but in other directions he was quite tame, and while his teammates and the Philadelphias were slugging away at each other, he stayed on the outer edge of the battleground.

He was, so to speak, at peace with the world and minding his own business when a Philadelphia man broke out of the brawling crowd, rushed up to him, clouted him on the jaw, and then plunged back into the main battle.

Big Joe was hurt, not so much from the clout as from the conduct of his assailant. "I wasn't hitting anybody," he complained later. "What did he want to come up and slug *me* for?" His question was answered when someone approached the man who had hit him and asked for his reason.

"I was in there," said the Philadelphia player, "slugging away at whoever was handy, and I happened to look up and there was Big Joe standing off to one side. I happened to think about his wild pitching, and how a couple of times he hit me in the ribs with his fast ball, and so I decided I'd do a little hitting on my own. So I just ducked over there and popped him one."

IN THE TOWN of Amenia, New York, a vigorous citizen named John Bide was chief of the fire department. John also was an outfielder and star hitter for the local baseball club. On an afternoon in 1934 Amenia was playing host to a team from Poughkeepsie. Early in the contest John Bide slammed a double to give his team a one-run lead. Amenia was having a tough time holding that lead, because the Poughkeepsie stickmen were walloping long ones to the outfield. John Bide was puffing after having hauled in a tremendous Poughkeepsie drive when a fire didn't have any more sense than to break out somewhere in town. The siren screamed and Fire Chief Bide started running again, this time toward his automobile. Passing the Poughkeepsie bench, he slowed down. "Goin' to the fire!" he called out to the visiting manager. "How about lettin' me back in the game if I get here in time?" The Poughkeepsie skipper nodded.

The fire didn't amount to much and the chief was back at the park before the game was over. He arrived, in fact, just as the player who had substituted for him was stepping to the plate, with a man on third. Fire Chief Bide pushed him aside, faced the pitcher, and belted a single that broke a tie and won the game for Amenia.

Sounds almost like a movie, doesn't it?

A CERTAIN UMPIRE working the Southern Association circuit found himself, one day in 1938, in Chattanooga with nothing in particular to do. Originally he had been scheduled, on this day, to officiate at a game in Knoxville, but word had come to him that the game had been moved up to a later date and here he was with some free time on his hands. He decided to take an umpire's holiday and go to a ball game.

Out at the park he settled himself in a seat, unrecognized by the fans, untouched by bitter arguments over close plays, and watched the Chattanoogas have at the Nashvilles. All in all it was an idyllic afternoon until, along about the fourth inning, he happened to glance out at the scoreboard. What he saw curdled his corpuscles.

"Great leaping balls of fire!" he exclaimed, for there on the big board was the score of the first two innings between Knoxville and Birmingham, playing at Knoxville—the very game he was supposed to umpire, the game he believed had been postponed. He was a conscientious man, so, fighting off his sickish feeling, he dashed to a telephone and spent the price of a steak calling Knoxville. It took a little time but finally he got someone in authority on the phone and was assured that no ball game was being played that day in Knoxville.

He found the answer a bit later. Joe Engel, the playful boss of the Chattanooga club, had spotted him in the stands before the game started. Engel knew about the postponed game, but he rigged it with the boys who handled the scoreboard to post a phony score, for the sole purpose of bewildering the ump. That Joe Engel is a whizzer. He's the same man who once traded an inept shortstop for a turkey, then roasted the turkey and served it to local sports writers who had been complaining about the maladroit infielder.

THE OFFICIAL RECORD of a game between Jersey City and Newark, played on May 25, 1946, showed that Buster Maynard, left fielder for Jersey City, had doubled off the left-field fence in the first half of the sixth inning. There was more to it than that, however.

The moment the play was completed the Jersey City players swarmed around Umpires Scotty Robb (what a name for an umpire!) and Arthur Gore. They contended loudly and with gymnastic gestures that the ball had gone over the top of the barrier and into the crowd, and then bounced back onto the field. It was, in their view, a home run.

The two umpires insisted that they had eyes, and their eyes had told them that the ball struck near the top of the wall, and that Buster's proper place was at second base. Ordinarily that would have settled the dispute, but the following day a Newark newspaper carried this report:

"Late yesterday the faces of Umpires Scotty Robb and Art Gore were a deep crimson. They learned the Maynard drive hit a youngster on the head before rebounding to the field. The unidentified kid was sent to a hospital for observation for a possible fracture. Nothing will be done about it, of course, but Maynard did hit a homer, not a double, and the Jersey City club might have won by a 4 to 3 score in nine innings, instead of losing by that score in eleven innings."

In Newark, it would appear, a mere skull fracture goes for a two-base hit. You gotta kill your party to get a home run.

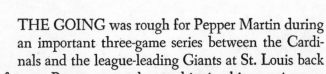

THE GOING was rough for Pepper Martin during an important three-game series between the Cardinals and the league-leading Giants at St. Louis back in July of 1935. Pepper got only two hits in thirteen times at bat during those three games, and his fielding was atrocious. In the second game he made three wild throws that let in six runs, and in the final contest he cut loose with another vagrant throw that gave the Giants two runs.

The fans, who have little tolerance for a faltering ballplayer, showered the often spectacular third baseman with abuse. It remained for one anonymous Cardinal booster to come up with the crowning indignity. After watching Pepper's wild behavior in the field, he slipped away from the park, found a drugstore and put in a call to the Cardinal office. Getting one of the club's officials on the phone, he said: "I'm calling for my sister who would like to get a job with you people." The official said there were no vacancies in the office. "It's not a job in the office I'm talking about," the caller said. "I think it would be to your advantage to hire my sister to play third base."

THE CLASSIC STORY about Babe Herman's son is the one in which Wilbert Robinson appears. The old-time Brooklyn manager took a strong liking to the child and often had him in the dugout, where the boy usually sat on Uncle Robbie's lap. Came the time when Papa Herman went into a horrible batting slump, and after he had gone hitless for almost a week, he turned up at the park with his son. The child went immediately to Uncle Robbie and climbed into his lap. Uncle Robbie promptly growled and brushed the boy off, all but knocking him to the floor. The child stood there a moment, bewildered, tears welling in his eyes, and then Uncle Robbie shouted: "Ask your old man why ain't he hittin'!"

Less familiar is the tale of the time Babe forgot his son. On this day he took the boy to the park, Mrs. Herman being in the hospital expecting an addition to the tribe. Babe parked the child in a grandstand seat and gave him a lecture: "You stay right in this seat and don't move out of it till Papa comes to get you."

The game was a tight one, with Brooklyn winning in the ninth. When it was all over Babe broke for the dressing room, excited over the victory, zipped through the routine of showering and dressing, and headed for the hospital. Arriving there, Mrs. Herman called his attention to the fact that he had not brought their son and then, of course, Babe remembered. Back at the ball park he found the boy glued to that seat, obedient to the end.

Herman denied the story, as he usually denied stories dealing with his own eccentricity—that famous fly ball *did not* hit him on the head, it only hit him on the shoulder. This time he said he only got about two thirds of the way to the hospital when he remembered his boy was still at the park.

THE NAME OF JOE KING is not on the roster of Baseball's Hall of Fame, and rightly so. We have reference here to Joe King of Denver, not Joe King the sports writer. There should be, however, some sort of a secondary hall of fame to accommodate men of achievement in the category of Joe King. Maybe it could be called the Hall of Ill Fame.

Joe was playing left field for Denver in a game at Omaha on August 3, 1947. Ed Lewinski was Omaha's star with the stick and early in the contest Ed whaled out a homer. In the eighth inning he got hold of another one and it all but disappeared into the welkin.

Out in left field Joe King watched the ball, saw that it was going over the screen on top of the left-field fence. But Joe had been anticipating just such a situation, and was prepared for it. He had a spare ball in his pocket. He pretended that the ball hit by Lewinski was fieldable. Racing at full speed toward the fence, he slipped the ball from his pocket and, as he came up to the barrier, tossed it against the screen. As it bounced back onto the field, Joe scooped it up and fired it to the infield before Lewinski could get beyond second base.

Umpire Joe Greene was had. Joe King's trick had momentarily deceived him. But not the Omaha manager. His sharp eyes had caught the play and he charged onto the field, and soon convinced the umpire, so Lewinski was waved on home. It was a good try.

OUT OF THE ancient newspapers comes the story of Silent John Titus and his toothpick. Silent John was a star stick wielder for Philadelphia in 1905 when the eastern team arrived in St. Louis for a series. He was noted for his flowing mustache, but more than that, he was famous for the fact that he always had a toothpick in his mouth when he stepped to the plate. "Without I'm bitin' on that ole toothpick," he sometimes said, "I ain't able to hit nothing past the pitcher."

J. A. McDougall was pitching for St. Louis when Silent John came to bat. McDougall was a man of temperate manner, but that toothpick had always bothered him. He got so he hated the sight of it—held firmly in the teeth of this prodigious hitter facing him there at the plate.

In this instance, McDougall's anger got out of hand. He took dead aim and threw a hard one, calculated to knock that toothpick down Silent John's gullet. Silent John dropped to the ground, evading the pitch. Then, instead of getting up at once, he started pawing around in the dirt. The ball hadn't hit him, or the toothpick, but the toothpick was gone. He remained down on all fours, scratching like a chicken. This went on for quite a while and then the umpire ordered him back on his feet. Silent John begged for just a little more time. He went over to the dugout. "Lemmy borry a toothpick," he pleaded, addressing his teammates. But no one had a toothpick, so Silent John silently returned to the plate—and struck out.

THE LEAVENWORTH CLUB of the Western Association had a bad year in 1948, finishing 27½ games back of the pennant winner. Both the fans and the management were unhappy about it, but looked forward to the next season with optimism. Things grew even worse, however, when the 1949 season got moving. The first week in May found the club with no victories and twelve losses. At this point President Robert Ricketson inserted an ad in a Kansas City newspaper, saying:

> Ballplayers wanted. Two outfielders and a second baseman. Must be eligible to play professional baseball in Class C. Call Leavenworth 34, or 1039W.

Mr. Ricketson got eight phone calls. Five were from genuine ballplayers. One was from a reporter. One was from a drunk. And the eighth was from a lady fan who said that after watching several games, she was certain she would be good enough to play for Leavenworth.

CASEY STENGEL has small respect for the master-minding he sometimes gets from the grandstand.

Casey will never forget the piece of violent criticism that reached his ears one day when he was manager of the Brooklyn Dodgers.

Brooklyn had the bases loaded with two men out and the pitcher due at the plate. Casey didn't like to send in a pinch hitter, because his pitcher had been doing well on the mound, but he needed runs so he made the decision: he told Babe Phelps to go up and hit for the pitcher.

Phelps did go up, and he also hit. In fact he belted the ball over the fence to give the Dodgers four runs. However, the opposition also did some scoring and the contest was close, as it went into the eighth inning.

In the last of the eighth Brooklyn needed runs. They managed to load the bases again and now the same situation arose —the relief pitcher was due to bat. Again Casey decided to use a pinch hitter. He stood up and surveyed his bench, trying to decide on a man to go up there and hit. He hadn't quite made up his mind when a foghorn voice belonging to a fan seated near the Dodger dugout assaulted his ears with these words:

"A fine manager you are, Stengel! If you haddena already used Phelps to pinch-hit you'd have him so's you could use him now! What a bum you are, Stengel!"

IN THE OLD DAYS the use of spikes as weapons both of defense and offense was much more common than today. There was a period of several years, however, from 1914 on, when almost no ballplayers were spiked in the New England area. Around 1912 a player named Genest, with the Springfield club, made a try at stealing second during a contest with Hartford. Infielder Jimmy Curry was waiting for him, and when the dust settled Genest was suffering from severe spike wounds in the leg. The injuries removed him from the line-up for the remainder of the season and were still giving him so much trouble the following season that he was unable to play. Ballplayer Genest decided at last that his career had been damaged, so he filed a suit against Curry. Thus it came about in 1914 that a Massachusetts court ruled that Mr. Curry would have to pay Mr. Genest one thousand dollars' damages for having spiked him out of organized baseball. The precedent having been set, ballplayers around New England were mighty careful after that just where they put their feet.

IN OUR EARLIER BOOK there were stories about batted balls landing in old tomato cans, in the smokestacks of locomotives, and in other odd receptacles. Out in San Francisco one day in 1947 the local team was playing Sacramento. It was San Francisco's game all the way, but the Sacramento boys never quit trying. Johnny Rizzo was batting in the fifth for Sacramento, with a chance to drive in some runs. He swung furiously at the ball, which rose high in the air, soaring back toward the stands. It was one of the highest fouls ever hit in the park and the catcher scampered back toward the box seats. It seemed to the spectators that that ball would never come down. Then there was a loud clang. It had arrived in the yawning mouth of a tuba belonging to one of the bandsmen.

FROM 1902 to 1909 Luther H. Taylor, a deaf mute, was on the pitching staff of the New York Giants. His affliction bothered him in only one direction—he was unable to give adequate expression to his opinion of umpires when they were wrong. It was his custom, at times when he was more than ordinarily displeased with a ruling, to indicate that displeasure to his teammates by use of the sign language. Some of the other players had picked up a smattering of the sign language through long association with Taylor, and understood what he was saying when he was calling the umpire bad names. Taylor came to grief, however, during a game in which he was pitching against the Cubs. The umpire gave Tinker a base on balls, and Taylor began saying shocking things with his fingers to his second baseman and shortstop. Suddenly the umpire came up beside him, tapped him on the shoulder, and thumbed him out of the game. The umpire, too, had acquired a smattering of the hand language.

BILL McKECHNIE, when he was managing the Cincinnati Reds in 1941, was a man given to deep concentration on the problems of the moment. One September evening when his team was scheduled to open a series at Pittsburgh, McKechnie stepped off a plane at the airport, deeply engrossed in the matter of which pitchers he would use in the series. Still mulling the problem, he made his way to a taxicab, climbed in, and muttered, "Forbes Field."

"Where'd you say?" the cab driver asked.

"Forbes Field," said McKechnie.

"It's a long ride if you mean the Pittsburgh ball park," said the driver.

"What are you talking about?" demanded the Cincinnati manager.

"You," said the driver, "happen to be in Detroit."

SEVERAL HUNDRED HUNGARIANS gathered at a Budapest athletic field one day in 1922 to see the first game of baseball ever played in their country. They had heard a lot about this game that was so popular in America and now they were going to see it firsthand.

One team was made up of members of the American Legation staff resident in Budapest. The other was composed of men from the American Consulate at Belgrade.

Bewilderment set in for the Hungarian audience right from the start. The Legation team came onto the field first, preceded by a goat. It was no ordinary goat, for it had been painted red, white, and blue. The Hungarian spectators were excitedly discussing this development, asking each other what part the gay goat would play in the proceedings, when the Belgrade players arrived, dragging two full-grown camels. Now the audience was really enthusiastic—this was going to be something! They were disappointed that the animals took no part in the actual contest, but were tethered on the sidelines.

The painted goat won from the two camels by a score of 20 to 1. When it was all over an American correspondent cabled home an account of the affair, which concluded: "Hungarian sporting writers were of the opinion that the game was too exciting for the Hungarian temperament, and declared that Magyar teams would be sure to leave too many dead on the diamond."

IF YOU SHOULD EVER be staying in a hotel where a ball team is housed and if you should observe one of its members prowling the lobby with his eyes on the floor, the chances are he's a hairpin ballplayer. For many years the hairpin has served as one of the most persistent of all baseball superstitions. A ballplayer who finds a hairpin is dead certain that he will get a base hit in the next game he plays. The origin of the superstition is clouded, but it dates back a long way.

Many years ago Frank Schulte of the Chicago Cubs was one of the devout believers in hairpin luck. One day Frank Chance, then managing the Cubs, got to talking with Schulte about hairpin luck. Chance wanted to know exactly how it worked. Schulte told him that finding one hairpin meant one hit coming up, and finding two hairpins meant at least two hits.

"What would happen," asked Chance, "if you found a dozen hairpins?"

Schulte ruminated for a few moments, having never considered this possibility, but he came up with an answer. "Well," he said, "the luck would sorta store up. You'd get a couple of hits every day till you run out the dozen and you'd be looking for more hairpins all that time, and if you found some, why, then you'd really have yourself one helluva hitting streak."

The most famous of the hairpin stories, however, begins in a five-and-dime store in Philadelphia. One morning a clerk in the store was mildly surprised when a middle-aged man approached him and asked for three dozen hairpins, plain.

The customer was a St. Louis sports writer, traveling with the Cardinals. The sports writer happened to be a close friend of Pepper Martin and had been grieving lately about Pepper's

43

batting slump. He knew that Martin was a hairpin ballplayer; he figured that the psychology of finding a hairpin might be the very thing Pepper needed.

Returning to the hotel, the sports writer scattered a trail of hairpins across the lobby floor from the elevator to the entrance. Then he sat down to await developments.

Soon the elevator door opened and out stepped Joseph Michael Medwick, sometimes called "Ducky." Medwick started across the lobby and then stopped, his eyes on the floor. He bent quickly and picked up a hairpin. Then he saw another. He dropped to all fours and began an eager harvest of hairpins —derned if it didn't look like half a dozen women had been in a knock-down drag-out fight the way the hairpins were scattered across the floor. The sports writer, of course, was upset. He hurried over to the crawling Medwick.

"Listen, Joe," he said, "please don't pick up those pins. Pepper is supposed to find them so he'll come out of his slump."

Medwick gave the writer a cold stare.

"The hell with Pepper," he said. "*I'm* finding these hairpins. Let Pepper find his own hairpins—these are base hits for me. You think I'm crazy?"

The legend goes that Medwick pounded the ball all over the premises that afternoon, while poor Pepper's slump continued.

ON THE FOURTH OF JULY, 1950, a man named Bernard Doyle was seated in the upper left-field stand at the Polo Grounds, one among 49,000 fans awaiting the start of a double-header between the Giants and the Dodgers. Suddenly Mr. Doyle slumped in his seat. A bullet had struck him in the head and where it came from no one knew.

This strange tragedy attracted wide attention and got page-one play in the newspapers. Yet it was not without a sort of precedent.

On a June day in 1947 the Reds were engaging the Cardinals at Sportsman's Park in St. Louis. It was an exciting contest and during the ninth inning there was a flurry of scoring on both sides and much whooping and shrieking from the fans. Amid all this tumult a spectator named Morris, sitting in the grandstand, felt a stinging sensation in his right leg. He looked down and saw blood. He left at once for a nearby hospital where an X ray showed a bullet lodged in his leg. Nobody knew where it came from.

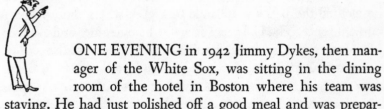 ONE EVENING in 1942 Jimmy Dykes, then manager of the White Sox, was sitting in the dining room of the hotel in Boston where his team was staying. He had just polished off a good meal and was preparing to light a cigar when two detectives came up to him and announced, "You've got to come with us."

Dykes gave them an argument, demanding to know why, but they wouldn't talk; they hustled him out of the hotel and down to police headquarters. Here he was led before the police commissioner himself. The commissioner was frowning, and spoke in grave double-talk for a while, then reached in his pocket and handed the Chicago manager a two-hundred-and-fifty-dollar watch.

A month earlier, when the White Sox were playing in Boston, Jimmy had been fined $250 for having, in the opinion of an umpire, tried to delay a game long enough to have it called on account of the Boston curfew law. Some of Jimmy's friends in Boston thought he had been given a rather rough deal, so they got together and bought him the two-hundred-and-fifty-dollar watch. He appreciated it deeply, but not the manner of its presentation.

THE MISTAKES made by base-line coaches are usually errors of judgment, originating and developing in the brain while the coach is standing in his normal position. There have been instances, however, in which coaching mistakes have been physical.

Years ago a basher of base hits named Beeline Beckman played with the Covington club in Kentucky. One afternoon he clouted the ball a town mile in a park where there was no outfield fence. The ball went far past the outfielder and Beeline Beckman, running hard, figured it for an inside-the-county home run. Arriving at third under a full head of steam, Beckman was just faintly aware of the fact that his coach was stepping forward to congratulate him. He slowed down a trifle to accept the kind words, and to allow as how 'twarnt nothing. Suddenly the realization came to him that the ball was on its way into the infield. He put on steam and started for the plate, tripped over the coach's feet, fell on his face, struggled off the ground, and wobbled his way into the plate just in time to be tagged out.

Yet another case involved the magnificent Wilbert Robinson, under whose aegis the words "Dodgers" and "daffiness" became synonymous. In the early 1920s the Brooklyns were playing the Pirates and the score was tied when the Dodgers came to bat in the last of the ninth.

Uncle Robbie was coaching off third when his catcher, Zack Taylor, caught hold of one and drove it deep into left center. It looked good for a home run. As Taylor came cruising around third his manager reached out and grabbed his hand, and then seized him by the shirt, and pounded him on the back, and all but kissed him. Meanwhile, the ball came in to the Pittsburgh pitcher, Wilbur Cooper. He snapped a quick throw to the third baseman. Zack Taylor was still in the congratulatory clutch of Uncle Robbie. He broke free and made a dive for the base, but the ball was waiting for him and he was tagged out.

THE BISHOP OF LIVERPOOL, England, got his name in the papers in 1937 when he viewed baseball with alarm. He said in effect that America's national pastime was no game for saintly individuals or even for sinners.

Writing in his diocesan review, the Anglican churchman said:

"In professional baseball the crowds play a vocal part to an extent unknown in any of our English games. The backchat and calls of both players and spectators at a baseball match in America are something to be remembered when the play is forgotten.

"So far English spectators of baseball have only learned the elementary calls of the game. If they ever learn the full phraseology of American baseball we do not think it will be long before its undesirable effects are seen at association football matches."

We recommend that the bishop come back for another visit, rig a concealed mike near home plate, and listen to the colloquy between Leo Durocher and, say, Umpire Lou Jorda. Might help him get a little more zip into his articles for the diocesan review.

AS LONG AS we're on the subject of Wilbert Robinson, let us for a moment abandon our resolution to steer away from Overlapping Anecdotes. The story of Uncle Robbie and the grapefruit has been printed many times, and remains one of the great tales out of baseball. The setting was Daytona Beach, where the Dodgers were training in 1916. Robbie was not exactly modest when he recalled his accomplishments as a catcher. One day he and a few of his players were watching an airplane flight over the beach. Ruth Law, the aviatrix, was making daily flights as a promotion stunt for a sporting goods store, dropping golf balls on a target. Uncle Robbie said he'd bet he could catch a baseball dropped from that airplane, and his boys snorted, venturing the opinion that such a ball would kill anybody who tried to catch it. Robbie then modified his boast, saying he could catch the ball if it were dropped from a height of about four hundred feet. The discussion grew warm and the Brooklyn players decided to goad their manager into carrying out his big brag. Miss Law agreed to take part with her plane the next day, and Frank Kelly, the Dodger trainer, said he'd go up with her and drop the ball.

Word of the stunt spread over Daytona and a large crowd was on hand the next day when Kelly and Miss Law took off. Robbie put on a mask and chest protector to keep himself from getting killed, donned a heavy mitt and stationed himself on the beach. The plane maneuvered a bit, then came loafing down the beach at the stipulated altitude and Kelly finally tossed out—not a baseball, but a large grapefruit. Down below Robbie staggered wildly around the beach, getting himself into position, and suddenly there it came—straight at his chest. He had his glove in position but the grapefruit shot past it, struck him in the chest, burst, and splattered its juice all over his head and neck. The force of the blow knocked him down and he sat there on the sand, his eyes tightly closed.

"Jesus!" he exclaimed. "Jesus, I'm killed! I'm blind! It's broke open my chest! I'm covered with blood! Jesus!"

When he knew the truth he cursed loudly and bitterly, fired

every ballplayer in sight, resigned from the club, resigned from the human race, and howled for someone to bring him a revolver. A while later, however, he had cooled off, and was saying:

"If it hadda been a baseball, by God I'da caught it."

"THERE WAS a dramatic conclusion to the baseball match, America *vs.* Australia, played at the Agricultural Show Ground on Saturday afternoon," the Sydney *Herald* reported one day in 1915. It came in one of the early innings when the Australian Minister for Health, a gentleman named Flowers, jumped from his seat, rushed onto the field and shouted, "Stop this silly game!"

In the second inning a ball had been fouled into the crowd. There was a scream and a call for a doctor, the ball having struck a woman on the head. She was not seriously hurt. A short time later another ball went into the crowd, hitting a man on the shoulder. At this point the Minister for Health decided it was time to halt the proceedings in the interests of public safety. Apparently he was the boss, for the game ended when he ordered it ended.

A NAGGING little mystery is bothering the authors of this book. It concerns a game between the Cubs and the Cardinals at St. Louis on a day back in 1915. In the last inning Umpire Byron called a St. Louis runner out at second. The runner put up a long beef and Umpire Byron thumbed him out of the game. This enraged the fans, to be sure, and they started throwing things at the umpire. They threw pop bottles, but mostly they threw cucumbers. Newspaper accounts of the matter said that cucumbers were flying onto the field from every section of the stands and bleachers. Nobody explained why the fans arrived on that particular day loaded with cucumbers. It is difficult to believe that word had been passed around the city of St. Louis: "Everybody show up at the ball park tomorrow and bring plenty cucumbers."

PERHAPS THE MOST celebrated vegetable barrage was laid down that disorderly day in 1940 when Detroit came into Cleveland to meet the Indians. The Cleveland fans were howling for vengeance. The Detroits had called the Clevelands "crybabies" and some other names. There was an almost constant shower of eggs, fruits, and vegetables from the stands, and the climax came when Birdie Tebbetts, then with Detroit, was knocked unconscious by a bushel basket full of tomatoes, thrown from the upper stands.

VIRGIL JENNINGS BARNES, who pitched for the Giants thirty-odd years ago, showed up at the park one day with a lame leg. John McGraw, knowing that Virgil hadn't hurt his leg on the field and always suspicious about such matters, demanded the reason for the limp. Virgil said he had slipped in the bathtub. McGraw said he didn't believe it—that in his opinion the pitcher had been out helling around somewhere. The Giant manager, in fact, inves-

51

tigated the story and determined to his own satisfaction that Virgil had *not* slipped in any bathtub. Then he slapped a fine of $100 on the pitcher.

A one-hundred-dollar fine was a heavy blow to a ballplayer in those days, and it hurt Virgil worse than the leg, but only for a little while. The story of the affair got into the newspapers and a man who manufactured rubber mats to prevent slipping in bathtubs read it. He promptly got in touch with Virgil and paid him $150 for an endorsement of his non-slip mats. Crime never pays.

THE EASIEST GAME Elwin "Preacher" Roe ever won was the contest on May 5, 1946, between Brooklyn and Pittsburgh. The Preacher made one pitch and his name appeared in the box score as the winning pitcher. Roe was with the Pirates that year. The game was tied at 3–3 with Brooklyn batting in the top of the ninth. Called in from the Pittsburgh bull pen, the Preacher found Ramazzotti on third base with two out.

The next Brooklyn batter stepped to the plate and the Pittsburgh catcher, Bill Salkeld, went into his crouch. He glanced down the third-base line at Ramazzotti and he either caught an opposition signal or had a hunch. At any rate, he signaled for a pitchout. Roe wound up and sure enough, the squeeze was on. Ramazzotti broke for the plate, the pitch came in wide, and Catcher Salkeld tagged the runner for the third out. In the last of the ninth Pittsburgh scored a run to end the game.

Roe's one-pitch victory was not without precedent. In fact Nick Altrock once won a game without throwing a single pitch up to the plate. Altrock was brought in at a tight moment in a White Sox game, with two out and a man on first. Nick's first throw was not to the batter, but to first, and he caught the runner off, ending the inning. The Sox then won the game in the last of the ninth.

SERIOUS DRINKING has all but disappeared among modern ballplayers, at least during the active season. A few years back we can recall the case of a big-league catcher who joined Alcoholics Anonymous in an effort to square himself around and retain his job. And a few years before him there was a famous outfielder who, it was said, couldn't get a proper perspective on a pitched ball unless he was looking at it through eyes grown slightly glassy. He was the man who one afternoon slood into second and came off the ground cussing, having busted the pint in his hip pocket.

Back around 1930 one of the problem boys of baseball was Flint Rhem, pitcher for the St. Louis Cardinals. On one occasion he disappeared for two days. Finally he turned up, appearing sheepishly in the presence of the Cardinal manager, Gabby Street. He looked more than a little worn and bedraggled, but he had an explanation—an excuse that has a classical ring to it. Rhem told Manager Street that gangsters had kidnaped him, locked him in a room, and forced him to drink horrifying quantities of liquor at the point of a gun.

In earlier times ballplayers put in almost as much time drinking as they did playing ball. Back in 1910 a Louisville liquor dealer acquired some publicity by announcing that he would give a certain local pitcher one case of whisky for each game he won. It was considered a nice gesture but actually it wasn't. The pitcher won nineteen games and got no whisky, for the reason that he scorned the offer, being a foe of booze—a fact which the liquor dealer knew from the very beginning.

LET THEM TALK of the restlessness of the retired firehorse, or of the strange power of printers'
ink. Baseball people say there is nothing to compare
with the magnetic power of the national pastime, once a fellow's
had a taste of it. The story of Tom Glennon is a case in point.

Tom was a young man playing organized ball on the Eastern
Shore of Maryland in the 1930s. One evening at a party a concert pianist heard Tom sing and told him he might have quite a
future in that direction. So Tom quit baseball and began studying voice under such men as Sylvan Levin and Dr. Herbert
Graf. He spent three years in the army and then, at the end
of the war, made his debut in *La Bohème* at the Academy of
Music in Brooklyn. Thereafter he sang more than thirty roles
in 140 performances with resident opera companies and on
tour. Late in 1947 he hit Broadway with a role in *High Button
Shoes* and was on his way to greater things—but the baseball
bug was gnawing at him. Early in 1949 he gave up his singing
career and became general manager of the Natchez club in the
Cotton States League. He said he loved opera and the stage
and all that, but he simply couldn't stand being out of baseball.

SUPERSTITION is on the wane among ballplayers today, according to some observers, probably
because so many of the kids coming up have been
recruited from colleges and high schools. Many of these young-
sters, however, exposed to the influences of the older men, soon
acquire at least some of the cabalistic beliefs that have gone

with ballplaying for so long. There remain certain superstitious notions that are held by the entire membership of baseball clubs. Among them, of course, is the one which demands that no mention be made of the fact that a certain player is approaching some sort of record-breaking achievement.

A strong effort has been made to compel the radio and television announcers to respect this superstition. A pitcher, say, is halfway through a game without having given up a hit. With few exceptions, the broadcasters make no mention of the fact that the pitcher is pointing for a no-hitter. Everybody on the field knows it. Everybody in the stands knows it. Everybody at home knows it. But it is not to be mentioned, even in a whisper. The only broadcaster we have ever heard in the act of deliberately violating the taboo is Red Barber. Red will do it by saying something like this: "I know a lot of folks are gonna be mad; I know a lot of you think I shouldn't do this, but in my opinion it's important, too important to ignore, and so I'm telling you, if you didn't already know it, that the pitcher out there on the mound has now gone seven and a half innings without giving up a hit." Red gets criticism from some of the players when he violates the tradition, but nothing like the abuse that comes to him from the fans. Heaven help him if, a few minutes after he has made his statement on the air, someone gets a hit off that pitcher.

The superstitions practiced by ballplayers on the diamond are but a small part of their traffic with charms and countercharms. A player in a batting slump spends all his waking hours devising little enchantments against the evil that has come upon him. Stan Musial, the great Cardinal hitter, has breakfast superstitions. When he gets into a slump, he tries reversing the order in which he eats the various items that make up his morning meal. Perhaps he'll hold off on his cereal until he's eaten one egg, then he'll eat the cereal and after that the other egg, and so on.

There are, too, a host of superstitions concerned with clothing. Bobo Newsom, arriving in the clubhouse before a game, always took his socks off in a certain fashion, swinging them by the garters above his street shoes, letting them drop into the shoes exactly the same way each day. Bobo believed, too, that the whole team would be jinxed if he tied his own shoelaces before going on the field. Always, after getting dressed, it was his custom to stand solemnly with arms folded while some other player knelt and tied the shoelaces.

IN THE DAYS when he was an outfielding star for the Athletics, Al Simmons arrived at a point in his career where he seemed unable to get a base hit under any circumstances. He tried all the traditional jinx busters with no success.

One afternoon, having lengthened his batting slump by going hitless in four times at bat, he headed for the clubhouse mad at himself and mad at the whole wide world. He was so preoccupied with his personal miseries that he scarcely knew what he was doing. He took his shower and toweled himself like a man in a trance and, walking naked to his locker, picked up his hat and put it on. Apparently a naked man wearing a hat is a comical sight, for his teammates began laughing. He advised them all to go to hell and, with his hat still on his head, sat down and began drawing on his socks. He dressed from the ground up and went on home to sulk, and the next day he got four hits.

For a long time after that Simmons pursued the same course in attiring himself—always starting with his hat as soon as he emerged from the shower, and his batting slump was definitely ended. Funny thing about it was—before long almost all his teammates were doing the same thing. It was possible to walk into the Athletics' clubhouse immediately after a game and find a couple of dozen men standing around naked with their hats on.

A SUPERSTITIOUS YOUNG MAN named Louis Bevilacqua was a pitcher for the Thomasville club in the North Carolina State League in 1941. Louis had a new superstition every day or two, never seemed quite satisfied with the one he was practicing and always was searching for a fresh method of invoking luck.

One afternoon a strange thing happened in the dressing room just before the start of a game. An outfielder was caught in the act of drawing a pair of ladies' panties, fashioned out of delightful silk, over his muscular legs. His teammates began ribbing him, but he was dead serious. "I gotta hunch," he said, "that these silk pants is gonna get me some hits today." He refused to explain where he had acquired the panties, or how he happened to get the hunch that they would be lucky for him. But they were. He went out that afternoon and slapped the opposition pitchers all over the lot.

The other boys continued to josh him about his dainty under-things, but not Louis Bevilacqua. Seeing, to Louis, was believ-ing, and he had seen those base hits. He decided that if silk panties would fetch base hits for an outfielder, silk panties might bring victories for a pitcher.

So it came about that Louis Bevilacqua acquired a pair of silk panties and began wearing them under his uniform. He won a mere seventeen games that season and, on the basis of his performance, moved up to the Chattanooga team in the Southern Association the following year.

A PLACEBO is a harmless and inactive pill which doctors sometimes prescribe for patients who only think they are sick and who insist that they need medication. Doctors recognize the fact that such pills often "cure" psychosomatic disorders. In baseball the placebo is called a "hitting pill." There have been a number of instances in which these pills have been employed to bring a player out of a batting slump; the most famous case is that of Paul Lehner.

When Lehner was with the St. Louis Browns he developed the idea that he could not hit the ball on Sundays. He had no religious scruples about playing on Sunday—he simply believed that Sunday was a bad-luck day for him.

He didn't talk about it, but it wasn't long before Bob Bauman, the club's trainer, found out about it. Bauman noticed that whenever it came time for a Sunday ball game, Lehner would approach him and complain of a sore wrist, an aching ankle, gastritis, or some other fancied ailment invented to keep himself out of the line-up.

At last Bauman got Lehner to unburden himself on the subject of his Sunday jinx.

"That's funny," said the trainer. "It just happens that I got word the other day about some new pills that are supposed to help hitters. Famous doctor discovered them. I've got some on order and when they get here, I think you and I ought to quietly give them a tryout."

Just before the next Sunday double-header, then, the trainer turned up with the pills. Lehner went behind a row of lockers and swallowed two of them. Then he went onto the field. In the first game he went to the plate three times without getting on base. He was beginning to doubt the efficacy of the hitting pills; then, coming to bat for the fourth time, he whopped a home run over the wall. In the second game he was a ball-of-fire at the plate. The hitting pills had cured him forever of the belief that he couldn't lay wood on the ball of a Sunday.

FOR THE SKEPTICAL READER, there's the case of Lou Novikoff and the hoopsa. Novikoff, the eccentric Russian who was attracting a lot of attention in baseball circles a dozen years ago, led the Pacific Coast League in batting during the 1940 season, finishing with a .363 average. He was red-hot, and the Chicago Cubs grabbed him.

In the opening days of the 1941 season Novikoff, in a Cub uniform, proved a major disappointment. He couldn't handle major-league pitching, apparently. His hitting was horrible. They were trying to figure out what to do with him when word arrived from his wife, still on the Pacific Coast, that she was heading for Chicago immediately and that she would have Lou hitting in no time at all. She informed the Chicago club that Lou could never hit unless he was eating hoopsa, prepared by her own hand. Hoopsa is a Russian dish, and Mrs. Novikoff said that so far as her husband was concerned, hoopsa and hits went hand in hand.

So she arrived from the Coast and went to work cooking hoopsa. In the next eight games Lou batted .173 and by the end of the season his average was an unspectacular .241. Hoopsa or no hoopsa, he was shipped off to Milwaukee.

FORREST ORRELL, pitching for the Detroit Tigers in 1945, nurtured a superstition which caused him no end of anguish. Somewhere in his career he awoke to the fact that he always pitched a winning game just after buying a suit of clothes. He was in no position to buy a new suit every time he was scheduled to pitch. In fact, he had a problem, and he discussed it with some of his teammates. Someone suggested that maybe the Detroit management would buy him a new suit before each game if he could convince the front office that the expenditure meant certain victory. No, said Forrest, that wouldn't work. He, Forrest Orrell, had to buy the suit out of his own funds, otherwise the charm would be nullified. Someone else recommended that Forrest take his savings and go out and buy a whole damn haberdashery with maybe a couple of hundred suits in stock; under this proposal, he would be stocking up pitching victories to last him the rest of his ballplaying career and, at the same time, he'd be setting himself up in a nice business. No, said Forrest, *that* wouldn't work—he had to buy the suits and wear them. He brooded about it for a long while and finally hit upon a possible solution. If a new suit of clothes would insure him a victory on the mound, perhaps a new pair of shoes would do the same. He might be able to afford a new pair of shoes each time he pitched.

On the morning of a day when he was to face the Boston Red Sox, Forrest went out with high hopes and bought a new pair of shoes. Later he stood on the mound and faced the Red Sox sluggers. They simply rained balls into the stands and Forrest was yanked in one of the early innings, and Detroit lost the game.

Forrest never even tried new socks after that.

DURING SPRING TRAINING in 1944 the Pittsburgh Pirates looked good. The whole team was hitting like mad in exhibition games. Two years later the Pirates were in a bad batting slump and Frankie Frisch got to thinking back to that 1944 training period. He consulted around among the more superstitious Pittsburgh players.

"It was that young fella," he was told, "that hung around the training camp with that mouth organ. Remember? Played it all the time. Always did say that fella brought us all that luck."

Desperately in need of a cure for his team, Frisch sent somebody to get the young fella with the mouth organ. He was brought on to Pittsburgh and told to start blowing. The first day he blew, the game was rained out. The second day he blew, the game was rained out. The third day he blew, the Pirates were beaten by an overwhelming score. The fourth day he didn't blow—Frisch gave him his unconditional release.

OF ALL THE daffy superstitions ever connected with baseball, the one cherished by Clark Griffith in his Chicago pitching days was the daffiest. Griffith believed that horrible luck would come to him if he pitched a shutout. Wherefore, when he appeared to be heading for such an achievement, he'd beg his teammates to ease up and let the opposition score a run, lest the special curse descend upon him.

LEFTY O'DOUL'S GLOVE was the key to his hitting ability. At the conclusion of each inning in the field, he'd take it off and toss it to the ground with a whirling motion. If, when it landed, the thumb was pointing toward right field, Lefty would get a hit the next time he came to bat.

EDDIE COLLINS, when coming to bat, would remove a large wad of gum from his mouth and stick it on the peak of his cap. If the pitcher got two strikes on him, Eddie invariably snatched the gum from his cap and popped it into his mouth. If he didn't do it, he said, the next pitch was a certain strike.

JOHN TITUS, outfielder for the Phillies many years ago, had a grand mustache. When the club went into a long losing streak, two of John's teammates, Sherwood Magee and Otto Knabe, decided that John's mustache was responsible. They asked him to shave it off and he refused, denying vehemently that it had anything to do with the team's luck. Magee and Knabe issued an ultimatum—either John shaved it off himself or, three days hence, they would throw him down and remove it. During the next two days Magee and Knabe made life miserable for Titus, spending all their spare moments honing large razors in his presence. He concluded finally that they meant business and, rather than suffer the indignity of losing his mustache by force, he shaved it off. The Phillies promptly came out of their slump . . . but poor John Titus appeared to have inherited all the bad luck that had belonged to the entire team. He couldn't hit and he couldn't catch flies and one night he fell out of bed and he lost a ten-dollar bill and he got a toothache. Magee and Knabe finally relented, and said John could let the mustache grow back. When it did, he was his old self, and the new mustache didn't seem to jinx the team, so everyone was happy.

BACK IN 1890 the streetcar company in Sioux City, Iowa, issued metal badges to members of the local ball club, entitling them to ride free on the company cars. Each badge was stamped with a number, and one of these was "13." The first man to have it was Joe Fitzgerald, a pitcher. He was released by the club within a month. It was given in succession to Bill Widner, Henry Siebel, Joe Crossley, and Robert Black, and every one of these men was sold down the river. Finally eight of the team's players formed a committee to devise ways and means of getting rid of the joner. The committee met in a saloon and, after lengthy preliminary discussions, moved in a rather wobbly body down to the bank of the Missouri River. A speech was made, a song was sung, and an outfielder with a powerful throwing arm took Badge 13 and hurled it far and away into the waters of the Big Muddy.

BILL MURRAY, manager of the Jersey City club forty years ago, got off the bench one day, placed a chair out in front of the dugout and sat out the game in the sunlight, believing that the change might help pull his team out of a long losing streak. Jersey City won the game. Murray decided that from now on he'd sit in the sun, and win ball games galore. The next day he was on the chair, and the temperature went up to 100°, and edged a trifle higher than that. The sweat rolled off Manager Murray, and the Buffalo ballplayers rolled across the plate, scoring run after run. In the seventh inning, with Murray on the verge of collapse from sunstroke, Buffalo scored seven more runs. That was enough. Murray got up, kicked the chair to pieces, and returned to the shade of the dugout. Any ballplayer who was superstitious, he growled, was plumb crazy.

FROM VARIOUS SOURCES we have been able to compile a small list of items that have been carried around and cherished by ballplayers in the belief that they were enchantments. They include:

> An old detective's badge.
> A short piece of trolley wire.
> A peach stone.
> A shred of red ribbon from a W.C.T.U. banner.
> A horse chestnut.
> The minute hand of a watch.
> A slate pencil.
> A rook from a chess set.
> A hotel key.
> A mandolin pick.

LEFTY GOMEZ was delighted one day when someone came to him with a handkerchief which Rube Marquard, the great Giant pitcher, had carried in his hip pocket during the period he was winning nineteen games in a row back in 1912. Lefty borrowed the famous handkerchief and tucked it in his own hip pocket. He lost the next three or four games in a row, miserably, then returned the handkerchief to its owner, with recommendations for disposal.

CASEY STENGEL is kidded about many incidents out of his past, including the time he forgot his pants. This matter dates back to the period in which Casey was managing the Toledo Mud Hens.

Throughout his managing career Stengel has been famous for his pre-game talks. He is often, as the saying goes, carried away by his own eloquence as he addresses his players in the clubhouse. On this day in Toledo he began his lecture before putting on his uniform pants and shirt. And when it was finished, it had been so compelling that Casey himself was spellbound. Studying his batting order, he followed his team onto the field, and the fans immediately set up a whooping. Stengel stood there a moment, wondering what all the shouting was about, and then he glanced down and found the answer. He was appearing before his public in colored shorts and undershirt. His retreat was not exactly hasty—it was a stampede.

DURING THIS SAME PERIOD Stengel gave an even more classic demonstration of his absent-mindedness. When the wheels of his mind were whirling on the subject of baseball, he was inclined to forget his surroundings completely.

Casey and the Mud Hens were in Kansas City, lodged at a hotel which was serving at the moment as headquarters for a big convention. The delegates to the convention were behaving in the traditional manner of delegates to conventions. The lobby was crowded all hours of the day and much liquor was being consumed.

The Toledo team returned to the hotel from the ball park

and Stengel's mind was occupied with thinking about a young outfielder who, during the game, had been responsible for a costly put-out. The boy had been tagged out at second because his method of sliding into the bag was all wrong.

Stengel came upon the young man in the crowded hotel lobby and called him off to one side to discuss the matter of the improper slide. Casey was not overly harsh about it—he just wanted to impress the boy with the nature of his sinfulness. He got to lecturing on the subject of sliding and in a few minutes he was under the spell of his own eloquence. He forgot where he was, forgot that he was in the crowded lobby of a big hotel. Glancing up, he saw a clear space between himself and a potted fern. The pot was approximately the size of second base.

"Here's what I mean," said Casey. "Now watch this closely —watch what I do with my right leg."

Then he launched himself across the lobby, full tilt, and went into a magnificent slide, hooking the potted fern with his leg.

Only then did Stengel realize what he had done. Embarrassment came upon him. He got slowly to his feet, a sheepish expression on his face. He expected that every eye would be on him, but when he raised his head and looked around, he discovered that nobody had so much as noticed his slide. The capers and conniptions of the tippling delegates had been so violent in the last couple of days that a mere hook slide into a potted fern made no impression whatever.

 A BRILLIANT PITCHING DUEL was in progress at Crosley Field in Cincinnati on the night of August 25, 1942. The great Carl Hubbell of the

Giants was pitted against Johnny Vander Meer of the Reds. The contest went into the fifth inning with Cincinnati leading 2 to 1.

Suddenly about three thousand fans left their seats on the first-base side of the grandstand and moved en masse around to the third-base side of the stand, where they remained for the duration of the game. This mass movement was preceded by an announcement over the public-address system, saying that it would be permitted. An eclipse of the moon was the reason for it. The eclipse began around eight o'clock but it wasn't much worth looking at until the fifth inning. Even then spectators on the first-base side couldn't see even a small slice of it. In as much as the crowd was small and there were plenty of seats on the third-base side, the management decided on the announcement. The management was a bit disgruntled in the first place —thousands of fans had stayed away, preferring to look at the moon without any distractions.

Vander Meer and the Reds won it, 3 to 1, and afterward a sports writer commented that "the Giants' eclipse could be seen from any seat in the ball park."

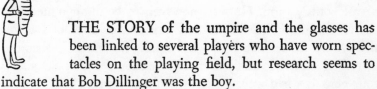 THE STORY of the umpire and the glasses has been linked to several players who have worn spectacles on the playing field, but research seems to indicate that Bob Dillinger was the boy.

Before he came up to the American League, Dillinger was playing with Lincoln in the Western League, back in 1939. He stood one afternoon at the plate and the ball came in and the umpire called it a strike. Dillinger thought that it had missed the strike zone by two parsecs. Without saying a word, he took off his glasses and extended them to the umpire. To

Bob's surprise the umpire casually accepted them, pulled off his mask, put them on, replaced the mask, and then bellowed, "Play ball!" Dillinger had no alternative but to turn and face the pitcher. The next ball streaked in. "Strike three!" quoth the umpire. Then he handed the glasses back to Bob.

THE CUSTOMARY opening-day ceremonies were being held in the Columbus (Ohio) ball park back in 1944. Nick Cullop, the Columbus manager, was in the dugout when someone told him he was wanted at home plate. "What for?" demanded Nick. "They're gonna make you a present," he was told. "No, by God," said Nick. "Those jokers don't get *me* a second time."

The year before he had responded to the call, and gone to the plate for impressive presentation ceremonies. The Columbus fans had presented him with about three hundred baby chicks. At the time Nick thought it a mighty fine sort of gift, and spoke his gratitude with feeling, and shipped the chicks home, envisioning himself as some day becoming proprietor of a vast poultry farm. He was, however, to be disappointed. As the chicks grew Nick got reports that all but three or four of them were roosters. It is said by experts in animal husbandry as well as economic analysts that possession of 296 roosters and four hens is a bad way to start a poultry business.

Now they were calling for Nick at the plate again, and he balked, and kicked the bench a couple of times, but finally they lured him out of the dugout and made another presentation. This time Nick's heart was really happy, for his gift from the fans was an enormous carton of chewing tobacco—enough to last him the entire season.

THE AUTHORS of this book would greatly enjoy getting the chewing-tobacco concession, or franchise, covering the big leagues in baseball, even in this year of 1951. We have no statistics separating the tobacco chewers from the gum chewers in the major leagues, but the evidence of the eye would seem sufficient. Even some of the kids brought up to the big time from high school baseball soon appear on the diamond wearing large lumps on their cheeks. Among the players themselves there is much ribbing back and forth between the partisans of tobacco and the adherents of gum. The tobacco boys accuse the gum chewers of being henpecked: "Ya wife won't leave ya chew, that's th' reason." The gum chewers in turn charge the tobacco men with slavery to "a filthy habit." It's all fairly good-natured though sometimes the cleavage gets serious.

A couple of years ago a rookie outfielder was brought up by one of the New York teams. He announced himself as strongly opposed to ballplayers who chewed tobacco. He began to complain to the manager about the spitting. He was told to take his Juicy Fruit and go somewhere and sit down.

One afternoon this rookie came down from third, headed for a close play at the plate. He came in standing up when he should have been sliding, and was tagged out. Back on the bench the manager ripped into him, but the young man was unperturbed. He let the boss rage for a while, and then said: "Now, just a minute. I warned you. All those dirty bums stand there at the plate and spit up toward third. Some of them spit between every pitch. I *told* you something would have to be done about it. I don't intend to slide into that mess. Long as you let it go on, I'll *never* slide!"

Back to the minors went he.

DAZZY VANCE, in his days as Brooklyn's star pitcher, threw harder and carried more chewing tobacco in his hip pocket than any other player on the club. Standing on the mound in the midst of a game, no matter how tense the situation might be, the Dazzler would interrupt matters now and then to install a new wad in his cheek. It was his custom to tuck the baseball into his armpit, haul his package of chewin' out of his hip pocket, freshen his wad, return the package to his pocket, take the ball out of his armpit, and dazzle them.

One afternoon the opposition worked a runner around to third. At this point Dazzy felt the need of livening up the tang of his cud. He went into his customary routine. He had the ball in his armpit and his package of tobacco in his hand when the runner suddenly broke for the plate. Dazzy had no time to consider what a scurrilous trick was being played on him. He had to do something and he had to do it rapidly. He hauled back and let go with the tobacco package. His catcher was startled, of course, but he grabbed the package and slapped it on the runner as he came in. "Safe!" announced the umpire and for a moment it looked as if Dazzy was going to beef; but he reflected a moment or so, and said to himself, "Well, there's two ways of lookin' at it, and I suppose if you look at it one way, he was safe."

WHEN HONUS WAGNER hit the majors he was assigned to first base. He could handle a sizable chaw, and did. One afternoon he walked to his position for the start of a game. He had his glove tucked under his arm and one of his huge hands was in his hip pocket, reaching for his tobacco. Suddenly things began happening. The pitcher had delivered to the plate and the batter had hit a ground ball to third. Wagner's hand was still in his pocket, surrounding the package, and somehow he couldn't get it out. He raced for the base, however, and as the third baseman's throw arrived, caught it with his bare hand—the free one. The put-out was made without his ever getting that other hand out of the pocket.

A PHILADELPHIA sports columnist dwelt upon romantic matters as he composed his daily essay one evening in June of 1933. He wrote:

"Bill Jurges of the Cubs was married yesterday morning to Miss Mary Huyette, of Reading, and he might do well to repeat the ceremony daily. The Chicago shortstop had the best day he ever staged here. After collecting a couple of hits in the first game of the double-header, which was featured by his brilliant fielding around short, he came back for a really fine batting display in the nightcap. He swatted Holley for two singles and a home run into the left-field bleachers and then beat out a bunt off Liska to make it four out of four."

The box scores for the games show that he also stole two bases and handled eighteen chances in the field without error.

ROSS BADGER, an umpire in the Pony League, had the affection of the fans at Jamestown, New York, for at least one day—July 10, 1945. Badger was married to Lucy Hubbard in a ceremony at home plate with three thousand fans, who paid to get in, looking on and cheering. A purse of several hundred dollars, collected from the fans, was presented to the newlyweds.

IF ANY BALLPLAYERS get the idea that a wedding brings immediate good luck, let them consult with either Warren Spahn or Mort Cooper. Spahn pitched against the Giants the day following his marriage and was sent to the showers in the fourth inning. Cooper got married one afternoon, pitched that night, and was knocked out of the box in a hurry.

DIXIE WALKER had the distinct pleasure one afternoon of catching his own home run. He walloped the ball into right field where it stuck in a wire net above the wall. At the conclusion of the inning Dixie went out to take his fielding position in right field, gave the fence a good shaking, and when the ball fell out, caught it and put it in his hip pocket.

SOME THEORISTS suggest that it is a healthy maneuver for a ballplayer to make a try at stealing second early in a game, for if he succeeds other players will be inspired to have a go at it later. The power of suggestion, the old college try, the competitive spirit, and other pseudo-psychological considerations enter into it.

Second base has been stolen twice, to our knowledge, without either steal ever getting into the record books; and in the second case, the person who stole the base was almost surely inspired by the first.

One of the World Wars was in progress when the Buffalo team of the International League played an exhibition game at Jamestown, New York, in 1943. The game was played at night and was in the middle innings when a siren screeched and a city-wide black-out brought pitch darkness to the ball park for several minutes. When the all-clear sounded and the lights went on, second base was gone. Somebody had sneaked out, unfastened it from its moorings, and made off with it. The officials dug up a substitute, put it in place, and the game was resumed.

Not many days after that, second base was stolen from the playing field at Lancaster, Pennsylvania, during a black-out called while the home team was playing York. A newspaper item about the Jamestown theft had appeared recently in Lancaster. In this case the game was delayed a half hour before a new second base could be located.

THERE'S A TOWN in Texas where, several years back, a bitter political situation existed. The reigning sheriff and one of the deputy sheriffs were at violent odds. The two men, in short, hated each other. For this state of affairs, Umpire James Kendricks was to become most thankful.

Kendricks was an umpire working in the East Texas League. During a game in this particular town one afternoon, he rendered a decision against the local team—a judgment which incited a large portion of the crowd to riot. They came pouring out of the grandstand, bent upon rending Umpire Kendricks limb from trunk, and leading the mob was no less a personage than the sheriff.

Just as the bellicose fans were closing in on Kendricks, the deputy sheriff came bulling his way to the side of the umpire. Drawing his revolver, the deputy confronted his enemy the sheriff and the rest of the angered crowd. "Anybody moves another inch," cried the deputy, "and I'll blow a hole in 'em you can see daylight through!" Nobody moved another inch. In Texas when a man makes a statement of that nature, it is said that he quite probably means business. The deputy forced the mob back, then cleared a path with the gun still in his hand, and whisked Kendricks off to the railroad station where the umpire just managed to catch an outbound train.

Kendricks never did find out how the political situation in that town finally resolved itself. Said he didn't much care.

WARTIME SHORTAGES prevailed throughout the nation during the 1945 baseball season. Members of the Memphis Southern Association team were as much aware of conditions as anybody else.

Among the Memphis players were George Morgan, shortstop, and Omar Lane, first baseman, and these two were roommates. The room they occupied contained one single bed and an extra mattress for use on the floor. In deciding which one should get the bed, the two boys came to an interesting agreement. The one who got the most base hits in the day's game would get to sleep in the bed. This contract had an important effect on the fortunes of the Memphis club. Omar slept on the floor considerably more than George. The first baseman got 47 hits in 48 games, whereas the shortstop whacked out 91 hits in 69 games.

OF DUTCH LEONARD'S knuckle ball the sports writers used to say: "Half the time he himself doesn't have any idea where it's going."

It was a tricky pitch, all right, and Dutch was using it one evening against the Athletics at Griffith Stadium in Washington. And one of his knucklers, thrown down to Hall of the Athletics, certainly arrived at a destination which was a great surprise to Dutch. The incident was described by a sports writer:

"Hall lined the ball back to the pitcher's box and Leonard

went into a sort of frantic dance. He couldn't find the ball. It had torn through his britches and disappeared into the recesses of his uniform. Before Leonard could dig the ball out from around his left knee, Hall had crossed first base with a single to his credit."

One detail was lacking from the account. Dutch Leonard said a swear word.

THE SPIRITS of all pitchers, of course, burgeon mightily whenever they chance to get base hits. A pitcher who has hit safely is a man suddenly suffused with great warmth and gratitude, loving the world and all its inhabitants, full of tolerance and good will and the urge to embrace humanity.

Take the case of a pitcher named Witt Guise, who was on the Cincinnati mound staff back in 1941. Witt was a lousy hitter. There were occasions, rare indeed, when he did manage to slop a hit off a right-hander, but he sometimes remarked sadly that he couldn't remember ever having hit safely off a southpaw.

Cincinnati came into the Polo Grounds and faced the king of the left-handers, Carl Hubbell. Witt Guise came to bat, automatically out, in his own mind. Hubbell got a two-and-two count on him and then Witt, making a listless pass at the next pitch, knocked it through the hole between second and first.

Never was there a more jubilant man! He talked about nothing else for hours. He was still talking at the dinner table that evening.

"A man like me," he said, "getting a hit off Hubbell—it's a miracle. I got the ball—gonna save it to show people—the one

76

I hit off Hubbell. Lord, what a good feeling! I just feel like doing something good for somebody. Believe I will!"

So he got up and went out to the hotel lobby and addressed an envelope and sent a dollar to the Salvation Army.

A CLERGYMAN suffering from saddle sores might not be considered cause for wide comment, but a clergyman suffering from saddle sores on account of a baseball game is worthy of attention. Back in July of 1943 the White Sox and the Dodgers were scheduled to meet in an exhibition game at Cooperstown, New York, the national baseball shrine. Down at Delhi, New York, forty-five miles to the south, the Reverend Thomas J. Carlisle, pastor of the Second Presbyterian Church, had a devout yearning to see that game. Owing to the war, gasoline restrictions forbade his driving up to Cooperstown. So he climbed on a bicycle and set out. Altogether he was about six hours on the road and when he reached home he announced it was worth it.

SOMETIMES after a ball game there are fans who are purple with rage; there are others who are red from embarrassment, and still others who are pink from sunburn. Up at Boston, after the opening game of the Braves' 1946 season, there were three hundred fans who had green behinds. These three hundred stormed the club offices, pointing to their green bottoms and howling for restitution. It appears that the seats in one section of the park had been painted late and the customers had not been warned about it. The club paid the cleaning bills for all those affected.

ONE OF THE most remarkable "ground rules" in the history of the game was put in force on a sunny afternoon years ago at the Polo Grounds. A dirigible came floating into view during the game, causing considerable stir, for this was in the days when a dirigible was something to gawk at; moreover, it was in the days when there were no regulations about flying low.

The airship maneuvered around a bit, dropping lower and lower, and finally, arriving at a location a couple of hundred feet above the field, assumed a stationary position so that the people on board could watch the proceedings.

It was distracting to the players, and they complained, but Umpire Byron, who was in charge of the game, wasn't going to make himself look ridiculous by trying to order the thing off the premises. He did, however, see his duty in another direction. He started waving his arms wildly, calling for quiet, and when he got it he bellowed: "If a batted ball hits that whatchacallit, it goes for a ground-rule double!"

THE YEAR 1946 was the toughest season for umpires in the minor leagues. A bumper crop of rhubarb caused many of them to quit in disgust. In the case of the American League, the year 1936 and especially the month of August was the low-water mark for umpires in the opinion of two of them—Bill McGowan and George Moriarty.

On August 7 the two were working a game at Cleveland.

It was Ladies' Day and more than eight thousand shrieking, bloodthirsty members of the gentler gender were in the stands.

At the end of the third inning Umpire Moriarty took his whisk broom and stooped over to dust off the plate. When he straightened up he had a bothered look on his face. He motioned McGowan, who was umpiring at third, to come in to the plate. They exchanged a few words and then McGowan put on the chest protector. Moriarty then stalked off the field, walking somewhat in the fashion of an automaton in an effort to keep the split in the seat of his pants from showing.

Four days later McGowan was umpiring back of the plate at Yankee Stadium, where the Yanks were playing Washington. Just before the game started McGowan bent to whisk off the plate and the same sickening sound reached his ears. His britches had split, but he was a man of large conscience and devotion to duty, and he decided to carry on. He umpired in an upright position, like a Marine captain about to receive the Distinguished Service Cross, and he seemed unable to call anything but balls. Largely because of walks, the Senators scored five runs in the first inning, more than enough to win the game. The Yankees put up a holler about McGowan's ramrod stance, so he retired briefly and changed his pants. The Yanks contended for a long time afterward that the rift in McGowan's britches cost them the game.

A few years earlier in the Georgia-Florida League an umpire happily named Phony Smith heard the seam in his trousers give way just as the pitcher went into his windup. Smith was no McGowan. He didn't even wait to see the pitch, but scooted for the dugout. He was off, so to speak, at the crack of the pants. When he returned a few minutes later he was told that the batter had hit the pitch, popping to an infielder, and he ruled that the play was legal and went for an out. A magnificent rhubarb ensued during which a cloudburst hit the field, and Phony was happy to be able to call the whole thing off.

ONE DAY IN MAY of 1938 some boys were playing ball in a Brooklyn street. One of them made a wild throw and the ball crashed through a window in the house where a judge named Sabbatino lived. The kids scattered in a hurry, certain that they were in for trouble, but nothing happened. On the following day they were back at their game and this time a batted ball went through another window in the Sabbatino house. And again nothing came of it.

A week or so later in another section of Brooklyn a cop broke up a street game, chased and collared one of the boys, and hauled him into court. Magistrate Sabbatino was on the bench and listened to the cop's story of how he had been summoned by householders who objected to ball games in front of their homes.

Then Magistrate Sabbatino spoke:

"I played ball in the street when I was a youngster and my sons play ball in the street. So do other boys, because they broke two of my windows recently and it cost me a dollar seventy-five to have them fixed. There's nothing criminal about playing in the street—it's better than being in cellars or pool halls. Case dismissed."

IN THE Kansas-Oklahoma-Missouri League they still talk about the time Dave Dennis got so mad at an umpire that he caught fire. Dennis was catching for Miami and Umpire George Carney was working back of the plate. Carney called a ball and Dennis whirled around and started a violent argument. That ball, he yelled, had been a perfect strike. The catcher was really in a state and the veins on his neck were standing out and the language he was using was strong enough to kill small oak trees. Umpire Carney, accustomed to such outbursts, just stood back and let Dennis rage, knowing all the time how the argument was going to end. Then suddenly the umpire came to shocked attention. He saw smoke rising from the angered catcher.

Dennis himself was in such a lather that he didn't realize he was literally on fire. Umpire Carney, in fact, had to call his attention to it. Whereupon Dennis ripped off his chest protector, and then his shirt, amid a shower of sparks. A large hole had already been burned in the shirt but the fire had done little harm to the catcher.

The explanation was simple. During the previous half inning while his team was batting, Dennis had piled "the tools of ignorance"—mask, shin guards, and chest protector—in a heap on the ground near the dugout. A cigarette butt flipped by a spectator had landed in a fold of the chest protector and stayed there when Dennis buckled it on.

IT SEEMS a little surprising that we fought on the same side with Great Britain in World War I after what appeared in a British publication called *The Bystander* in 1914. The New York Giants and the Chicago White Sox were barnstorming abroad, and after playing a game in London, the sticky wicket writer for *The Bystander* had this to say:

> After seeing the Giants of New York beaten by the White Sox of Chicago, one came away with a

feeling that it was a pity that so
much skill should be expended on
so futile a game, and wondering
what our American cousins can see
in it. It must surely be something
invisible to our eyes.

According to English ideas, more
than half the joy of a ball game con-
sists in hitting the ball with something and hitting it fairly often. But
in baseball the "batter" is at such a
disadvantage as compared with the
"pitcher" that hits are few and far
between. In short, the balance between attack and defence, which is
essential to a good game, is lacking.

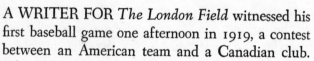

A WRITER FOR *The London Field* witnessed his
first baseball game one afternoon in 1919, a contest
between an American team and a Canadian club.
His published comment:

The American pitcher was so
deliberate in his methods as to be a
subject of wonder not unmixed with

admiration. He always walked to his place with extreme slowness, generally looked around three or four times if a man was at first base, raised his hands as if about to throw, dropped them, and twiddled the ball several times in his glove, swung his arms around in windmill fashion and, finally, when one had almost given him up in despair, threw the ball at the batter—if he did not throw it toward the man at the base.

Several times he began his duties by holding the ball at arm's length and standing motionless for some seconds, after which he went through the usual performance. Once or twice he altered his mind, signalled to the catcher, met him halfway, had a consultation, and went to give instructions to a field man before getting to work.

Yet baseball enthusiasts did not seem to recognise that there was anything slow about these things.

The British are truly a wonderful people, but they don't know nothing.

THERE WERE SOME who said the moon caused it. Be that as it may, sheer lunacy prevailed at Washington on April 26, 1931, when the Yankees played the Senators. That contest probably produced the greatest number of daffy plays per square inning ever witnessed in the major leagues. Let us piece together contemporary newspaper reports for the details:

Perhaps it was the conditions under which the game started, it being delayed fifteen minutes because of a heavy rain which was followed by a strong wind that seemed to send both players and umpires haywire. Whatever the reason, it was one of the weirdest affairs seen on a diamond within the memories of the oldest inhabitants.

First off the bat came one of those plays which Babe Herman has made famous in Brooklyn. After Lary had walked with one out, Cooke fanned. Then Lou Gehrig poled one into the stands in deepest center. The scorers lowered their eyes and started jotting down a homer for Gehrig and two runs for the Yankees. Now came the onset of madness. Lary came around from first, tagged the third sack with his foot, and then sauntered into the Yankee dugout.

Gehrig, however, came on around third and crossed the plate, whereupon Umpire McGowan ruled him out for having technically passed

Lary on the base path. Thus Gehrig lost his homer and was credited with only a triple. This third out retired the side and the Yankees lost the two runs which, as it turned out, represented the margin of defeat— the New Yorkers lost the game 9 to 7.

Gehrig's drive had landed in the stands and then bounced out. It was an obvious home run, yet Outfielder Harry Rice snatched it up and fired it in as if it were still in play. Lary must have thought the ball had been caught. His manager has probably told him to quit thinking in the future.

From then on everything that can go crazy in a ball game seemed to go crazy in this one. In the third inning the usually reliable Cronin let a Texas Leaguer drop for a hit. In the home half of that inning came one of the screwiest home runs on record.

Bluege sent a Texas Leaguer to right field and Dusty Cooke came in fast, trying for a shoestring catch. His spikes caught in the turf and he fell hard on his shoulder. He lay there in a semiconscious condition, the ball nestled in the grass a scant yard away. Gehrig came racing out for it, but Bluege was pounding around the base paths and crossed the plate with a legal homer. Meanwhile the whole Yankee team rushed out to the fallen Cooke, who was taken to a hospital with a displaced collar-bone and several torn ligaments.

This accident robbed the Yankees of a needed outfielder—the third out of a complement of five to be injured in the last four games, Ruth being hurt last Wednesday and Hoag last Friday. Ruffing had to be sent in as an emergency outfielder to replace Cooke and all afternoon Pitcher Ruffing added to the clownish confusion by refusing to hurry his throws lest he injure his pitching arm.

Later in the game Cronin was credited with a triple when Byrd fell down just as he was about to catch a fly; and Manush contributed to the chaos around third base for the reason that he thought there were two out instead of only one.

There were, of course, some classic collisions. Byrd and Lary crashed into each other, adding a fluke double to the fluke homer already credited to Bluege. And Spencer, the Washington catcher, charged all the way down to first base to succeed in knocking a pop foul out of Judge's glove.

Another time Fischer, the Washington pitcher, took a grounder, made motions to throw to several bases, and then got the ball over to Judge too late to nip the runner at first. Fischer's indecisive motions before making that throw seemed to confuse the Yankee base runners no end, because after Judge caught the ball too late to put *his* man out, he happened to glance across the diamond and saw two Yankees perched on third. Instead of throwing the ball, Judge simply ran across the infield and tagged one of them out. At this point Umpire Connolly took down with the fever, calling the wrong man out, so that he had to summon him back from the Yankee bench and put him on third again.

To add to all this there were more scratch hits than ever again will be seen in any one game, with balls dropping all around the feet of the fielders. And two Washington players were wild-pitched across the plate.

Umpire McGowan got back into the picture by staging a mind-reading act. In the ninth Chapman of the Yankees was batting, with two strikes on him. McGowan called the next pitch a ball. Catcher Spencer of the Senators turned quickly as though to protest the call. Umpire McGowan promptly ruled Spencer out of the game. When Spencer insisted he hadn't opened his mouth, McGowan agreed, and said he was exiling the catcher *for what he was thinking.*

Let it be noted that Lou Gehrig and Babe Ruth finished the 1931 season tied for home-run honors, each having hit forty-six. The ball Gehrig hit in that mad contest was as clean a home run as was ever recorded, yet Lary's mistake at third nullified it and it went into the books as a triple. Otherwise, Gehrig would have been the home-run king that year.

THE PITCH that McDonald Kerr threw that May day in 1946, when Birmingham was playing Nashville, may have been simply a crazy exhibition of anger and chagrin. Some say, however, that it was a clever stratagem.

Kerr was pitching for Birmingham, having been brought on in the second inning in an attempt to quell a Nashville uprising. He never did quell it, for the final score was 17 to 2 in Nashville's favor.

Tamulis, the Nashville pitcher, was the batting star. Four times he came to bat and hit safely. Pitcher Kerr was understandably displeased over this. Came the moment when Tamulis stood once again in the batter's box, and now Kerr departed from orthodox baseball. He reached down and picked up the resin bag, put his foot on the slab, and pitched the bag to the plate.

Umpire Steamboat Johnson, who was said to have started his umpiring career in the latter part of the sixteenth century, had never before seen a pitcher deliberately throw a resin bag to the plate. But Steamboat was equal to the occasion and promptly called a balk, and the Nashville runners moved up on the bases. Kerr didn't seem at all flustered by what he had done. He returned to pitching the baseball and two pitches later Tamulis popped it up for the only out he made all day.

EVER TELL YA 'bout th' time Hughie Critz made th' bird-dog deal at home plate? Well, sir, Old Charlie Moran, the same as umpired in the big leagues for over twenty years, he had this bird dog that he wanted to get rid of, and Hughie Critz had been talking a deal for a long time, but somehow they just couldn't seem to arrive at a final agreement. They'd come close to it, and then Hughie would pull away, and he'd tell Charlie he figgered he oughta think about it awhile. Charlie was getting mighty impatient about it, because he really wanted to get that bird dog offen his hands.

One afternoon it happened that Charlie was working behind the plate when Hughie came to bat. The count ran full on Hughie, three and two. He stooped over to get some dirt on his hands and while he was doing it, he turned his head around a little and spoke to Charlie.

"Charlie," he says, "I bleeve I've made up my mind. I'm gonna buy that bird dog a yourn."

Then he straightened up and the ball came in. The pitcher figgered he got the corner of the plate. Maybe he did. Several others allowed the ball was over. But Charlie Moran just hollered, "Ball four!" and Hughie trotted down to first. Seems like a funny place to be makin' a bird dog deal, don't it?

IT DOESN'T SEEM LIKELY that baseball will ever see the equal of the old Gashouse Gang, for which a triple alas and alackaday! When that wild and uncivilized band hit the road and stormed into one or another of the National League cities, strong men quailed and women and children hid in cellars until the invasion had been repelled.

Let us examine the impact made by the Gashousers on the staid city of Philadelphia back in the spring of 1936. The local newspapers chronicled the doings of the Cardinals as if Attila the Hun had ridden into town at the head of a barbarian horde. Said one paper:

> For three days this well-policed town has been prowled by a pack of unbarbered gorillas who looked as though they had just tunneled

their way out of the jute mill at Joliet.

The chipmunks nested in their beards. They wore overalls into the main food salon of one of the city's best inns. They preyed upon street carnivals and sacked and pillaged the midways. They frightened traffic cops with their hideousness and made movie cashiers reach for the ceiling.

They meant no harm. It was only the Dean brothers and the unspeakable Gashouse Gang trying to hex the Giants out of their winning streak.

The whole thing could have been hushed up. The cops had been fixed, the dog catchers had orders to stand by but to do nothing unless Pepper Martin and Durocher started to snap and bark.

But last night the lesser evil, Brother Paul Dean, declared himself as a public enemy and stamped into a carnival lot, smashing milk bottles with nickel rockets. The scandal broke.

And on the following day another paper reported:

Mr. Rickey must have appreciated his boys. Even though they grow a bit eccentric, wearing old clothes and refusing to shave until the New York Giants' winning streak is broken, they still keep on hustling on the ball field. Pepper Martin, in the thick of the scoring yesterday, has been wearing a set of whiskers these days. He looked like something off the House of David team.

But today the boys decided to doll up and shaved and changed their clothes before going to New York.

During that visitation the Gashousers spent one afternoon walloping the Phillies 11 to 6. That evening three men walked into the dining room of one of Philadelphia's fanciest hotels. They wore dirty overalls and greasy caps and carried hammers. They wandered unmolested around the swank room, pounding on radiators with their hammers, and nobody appeared to recognize them as Pepper Martin, Dizzy Dean, and Heinie Schuble. From the dining room they proceeded to the grand ballroom, where a convention of the Boys' Clubs of America was in session. There, in the middle of the convention floor, two of them faked a quarrel and then a free-swinging fist fight, which ended with Dean knocking Pepper Martin to the carpet. The kids were sharper than the splendid people in the dining room, and soon caught on, and compelled the invaders to get up and make some little speeches.

A NEW left-handed pitcher by the name of Clem Dreisewerd joined the Rochester ball club during spring training in 1941. The Rochester sports writers had been speculating about his ability and the club management predicted a brilliant future for the boy, provided his control held up.

On the day Clem reported to the club the manager asked him about his physical condition and whether he had kept his arm in shape during the winter.

"Oh, sure," said Clem. "I've been working out every day for the last six weeks. Edna's been catching me."

"Edna?" said the manager.

"Edna's my wife," said Clem. "She's as good a catcher as anybody I know."

The sports writers considered this matter worth a little further investigation. They learned that Edna Dreisewerd thought nothing of doing up the dishes, taking off her apron, pulling on a catcher's mitt and spending an hour working out with Clem. They learned, too, that she was a fine cook, that she weighed 116 pounds, and that she held the opinion that Clem's control should be a matter of worry to no one.

UMPIRE PAT PADDEN of the American Association was strolling down East Gay Street in Columbus one July afternoon in 1946. Suddenly, right there in broad daylight, he stepped into an open manhole. It wasn't a deep hole and Padden wasn't hurt, beyond a few trifling bruises, but the story of his fall got into the papers and brought him no end of embarrassment.

He had always been quite a ribber and now the ballplayers had him by the short hairs. "Always knew your eyesight was way off," they taunted him. "If ya can't even see a thing as big as a manhole, how can you pretend you can see a little old baseball comin' acrost the plate?" they badgered. Pat umpired the first game of a double-header that night and was supposed to work in the second game, but he withdrew and a substitute took over. Pat said he had a headache, but it was pretty obvious he just wanted to get away from it all, to get out of range of those ballplayers.

Within a few days of the Padden incident, the newspapers reported that Umpire Roy Funkhouser had submitted his resignation to the president of the Kitty League. A dead cow was given as the reason for his quitting. He had completed an umpiring assignment at Hopkinsville, Kentucky, and was driving his car to Mayfield when he hit a cow. The cow succumbed, Funkhouser's leg was hurt, and his car was smashed up. After the accident he got to thinking that if a man can't even see a cow on the open road, he's got no business umpiring ball games. And so he decided to resign.

DETROIT AND CLEVELAND were battling each other in a bitter pennant race in 1940 when a series between the two clubs opened at Detroit on the twentieth of September. It was pretty much agreed all around that the winner of this series would cop the pennant.

Detroit took the first game by a score of 6 to 5, giving them a big edge both statistically and psychologically. The Clevelands were extremely low in spirit as they returned to their hotel rooms that night. Among the morbidly depressed Indians were two young pitchers, Harry Eisenstat and Johnny Humphries, who happened to be roommates.

They slept fitfully through the night, tossing and groaning. Along about 2 A.M. Eisenstat got out of his bed and went to the bathroom. A few moments later Humphries awoke in the other bed. He glanced over and saw that Eisenstat's bed was vacant. Then his eyes moved to the window, which was standing wide open. A horrible thought came to him—his pal, brooding over the loss of that game, had leaped from the window to the pavement far below. Humphries scrambled out of bed and rushed to the window. He was leaning far out, trying to see some evidence of his friend's suicide leap, when Eisenstat came back into the bedroom. Now it was Eisenstat's turn to be astonished. Here was his friend, out of his mind from the loss of that game, on the verge of taking his own life.

"Don't, Johnny! Don't do it!" he cried. At the same time he rushed forward and grabbed Johnny. In a little while they got it all straightened out, and went back to bed, and even after Detroit won the pennant they didn't try to end it all.

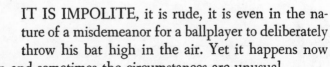 IT IS IMPOLITE, it is rude, it is even in the nature of a misdemeanor for a ballplayer to deliberately throw his bat high in the air. Yet it happens now and then and sometimes the circumstances are unusual.

Forty years ago Ivan M. Olson, an infielder for Cleveland, took vigorous exception to a strike called on him by Umpire Tom Connolly. Olson emptied his mind by way of his mouth at the umpire and, seeming to make no impression on the official, threw his bat high above home plate. When it came down, Umpire Connolly walked over and picked it up, without comment, and then *he* threw it high in the air—a good ten feet higher than Olson had thrown it. "See that?" spoke the umpire, in tones loud enough for even the spectators to hear. "You are no better at throwin' a bat in the air than you are at judgin' a pitched ball. Now go on about your business."

In the late 1940s at Mobile, an outfielder named Walter Sessi was so disgusted at having fanned that he heaved his bat into the air. Grumbling and grinding his teeth in chagrin, he started back toward the dugout and the bat came down and hit him a fearful clunk on the head. A knot rose on his noggin that made him look exactly like a man who has just been hit on the skull by a bat.

Another bat-throwing incident involved Danny Murtaugh, always a good infielder. He was playing for Houston back in 1940 and one afternoon, standing at the plate, had a count of three and two on him. He let the next pitch go by and the umpire called it a strike. Danny was in a fury. He threw his bat in the air and probably established an unofficial record for altitude. The bat was still going up when the umpire yelled: "You catch that bat when it comes down or I fine you twenty bucks!" Danny made a diving catch, saved himself twenty dollars, and then went on back to the bench, considerably more satisfied with himself.

CLYDE DAY, who played with Brooklyn once upon a time, was mighty proud of his remarkable chest expansion until it—the chest expansion—broke two of his ribs. Clyde had a parlor trick involving that expansion. First he'd borrow a belt from someone. Then he'd exhale, pull in his chest, and fasten the belt around the upper part of his torso. With the belt well buckled, he'd begin taking in air and almost invariably he'd bust the strap.

One evening some of the Brooklyn ballplayers were gathered at a small party. It needs to be said that most of the boys were pretty bored, by this time, with Clyde's belt-busting. "Him and his durn chest expansion," they'd say. "Seems like we can't get together any more without he's got to start puffin' that chest out and bustin' belts."

Well, on this particular evening they fixed him. One man had gone to a harness maker and had him rig up a belt that looked quite average but that a team of horses couldn't have broken. Sure as shootin', Clyde Day began bragging about his chest, and pretty soon he was asking for a belt, and he got one —the special job. He went into his act, got the belt fastened around his chest, and gave it a try. Nothing happened. Now he gave it everything he had—a deep inhale, a pause, and Clyde let go. His face turned purple and the veins popped out on his forehead, and a faint crack was heard in the room. Two of Clyde's ribs had snapped, and that was the last time, at least in that particular group, that he ever expanded his chest.

THE PORTLAND TEAM of the Pacific Coast League won its seventh game in a row on July 16, 1942, and then the bottom dropped out of the ball park, to a certain extent. The Portlands beat Oakland in the first game of a double-header. At the end of an inning and a half of the second game, Portland outfielder Rupe Thompson started in from center field when he felt a sort of trembling in the ground beneath his feet. He leaped backward and watched a hole about five feet in diameter open in the earth. Left-fielder Mailho came running over to see what had happened, and climbed down into the hole to see what the hell. Only the top of his head was visible once he was in it. He discovered that a drainage pipe line had collapsed, causing the cave-in. It took a half hour of hard work to get the hole filled up so the game could proceed.

The delay really saved Portland. Oakland was ahead 2 to 0 at the end of three innings, when the game was called off.

ORIS HOCKETT and Arnold Moser were playing the outfield for Nashville in a game with Knoxville one afternoon in 1940. A Knoxville slugger came to bat and even though the outfield was playing him deep, slammed the ball far over Center-fielder Moser's head. Moser turned tail and started running. As he sped over the ground he kept glancing backward and upward, following the flight of the ball. At last he gave a mighty leap in an effort to catch it. The ball hit the scoreboard and came down. Moser hit the scoreboard but he didn't come down. Moser's belt had caught on a stout peg used to fasten square pieces of tin in posting the score. And there he hung.

Oris Hockett, meanwhile, had come racing over from left field. He and Moser were close friends, and Oris was now in a momentary dilemma. His first impulse was to get his pal down off the scoreboard; on second thought he decided that maybe the ball was pretty important. He snatched it up and fired it to the infield in time to prevent the runner from scoring. Then he helped Moser get off the scoreboard.

THE GREAT YANKEE Bob Meusel once had two umpires pleading with him to confess, openly, that he had been thrown out at first base. New York was playing St. Louis and the two umpires involved were Bill Guthrie, working back of the plate, and George Hildebrand, on the bases.

Lou Gehrig reached first with two out and Umpire Hildebrand moved on down toward second, as was customary. Meusel was next up and hit a grounder toward shortstop. It looked like a cinch to force Gehrig at second and end the inning. Hildebrand got into position to observe the play at second, crouching with his back turned on first base. He saw the second baseman racing toward the bag to take the throw from the shortstop, and he saw Gehrig come sliding in to the bag. Meanwhile the St. Louis shortstop, recognizing the fact that Gehrig probably would beat the throw, turned and fired the ball to first.

Umpire Hildebrand, of course, didn't see the play at first. He assumed that his colleague at the plate, Guthrie, had seen it and would rule on it. But Guthrie hadn't. He had assumed that the play would be an easy force-out of Gehrig at second, and anyway he knew Hildebrand was on the job down there, so he had turned away from the field to replenish his supply of baseballs.

Now both umpires moved down toward first where Meusel was standing on the bag. Everyone else in the park, apparently, knew that Meusel had been thrown out at first by at least two steps—but the umpires didn't know it. They approached Bob with politeness.

"Were you safe or were you out?" Hildebrand asked him.

Meusel just smiled.

"Oh, come on now, Bob," said Guthrie. "Neither one of us saw it. Did that throw get you?"

"It's not for me to say," Meusel answered. "You guys are the ones that have to decide things like that."

They begged him to be reasonable and tell the truth, but he wasn't talking, and so they held a whispered conference, in which they decided they could do nothing but let Meusel have the base. The St. Louis players yipped and cussed about it, but got nowhere. And both umpires were thankful, a few minutes later, when the next batter popped out and got them off the hook.

BILL JACKOWSKI, an umpire in the American Association, could be just as stubborn as any umpire in the majors. Bill was working a night game at Columbus one night in 1949. The home team was ahead when it began to rain. A drizzle, then light rain, then a downpour. The fans bellowed for the game to be called, but Bill had no use for pressure groups. He'd call the game when he durn well felt like calling it. Still the rain came down and the Columbus players began to hector the umpire, who responded, "Shaddup!" Somebody hit a foul fly and Bill scampered toward first to rule on the play. Suddenly he went down, kerplop on his can, in the middle of a large puddle, splashing mud clear to the box seats. While the crowd roared its pleasure, Bill sat there for a few moments and then, before he ever got back on his feet, an official recess had been called.

THERE EXISTS a remote possibility that sports writers someday will have to alter a certain phrase that is fairly common in baseball stories. It would become: "He was off at the clank of the bat."

Back in 1944 Professor A. E. Drucker of the Washington State College School of Mines spoke before an engineering group at Spokane. He revealed that metal baseball bats were being produced in the laboratory at the college. These bats, he said, were made from magnesium and would be on sale at sporting goods stores within a few months. That's the first and the last we heard of them.

IN THE NATION'S CAPITAL on the afternoon of October 7, 1913, members of the House of Representatives were locked in their chamber while deputy sergeants-at-arms roamed the town trying to drum up a quorum.

In New York that same afternoon McGraw's Giants and Mack's Athletics were playing the first game of the World Series.

The imprisoned congressmen fretted and fumed, for it looked as if they'd have to twiddle their august thumbs all afternoon without knowing how the big game was going.

Representative Mann, the Republican floor leader, finally arose to state a parliamentary inquiry. "I wish to ask," he intoned, "if the Chair has made arrangements to inform the House of the progress of the game in New York?"

"That is not a parliamentary inquiry," the Chair ruled.

Some more time passed and then a messenger was admitted to the chamber. He hustled to the side of Congressman Mann and whispered something to him. Once again Mann informed the Speaker that he wanted to get a parliamentary inquiry off his chest.

"State it," said the Speaker.

"Would it be proper," asked the congressman, "for me to announce that the score is now 5 to 1 in favor of Philadelphia in the fifth inning?"

"Out of order!" boomed the Speaker, grinning.

"That being out of order," Mann resumed, "I ask if it would be in order to announce that Baker of Philadelphia has just hit a home run?"

Cheers sounded and nobody heard the Chair's ruling, and a little while later the House voted to let the quorum go to the region known as hell, and adjourned.

JUDGING FROM newspaper reports of the period, there was great enthusiasm in Dublin back in 1917 when a game of genuine baseball between an American and a Canadian team was scheduled at one of the city's athletic fields. One sports writer, whose specialty was cricket, divested himself of the following prose:

> The American and Canadian boys will reach town this evening, and they are as keen as mustard to give Dublin a good show. Mr. Lee, the hustling skipper of the United States bunch, completed the working out of the playing pitch this morning. He is charmed with the ground.

Belfast is sending a representative to get the hang of the game. Schoolboy and schoolgirl tickets are selling like hot cakes. At least one American gentleman has already crossed the Channel to see the game in Dublin tomorrow, for it is now known that both teams have trained to the last ounce.

ONE OF THE AUTHORS of this book has a wife-woman who refuses to attend a baseball game, or even to look at baseball on television, because of the strategic maneuver known as the deliberate base on balls. The first time she saw the maneuver—the catcher stepping to one side and the pitcher delivering beyond the reach of Joe DiMaggio, she said: "That's all, brother! To hell with that kind of a deal." Whereupon she took her departure, devoting her future energies to learning discords on the ukulele.

She is not alone in her dissatisfaction with certain regulations contained in the game. There was the case back in 1932, for example, of Hugo Bezdek, director of physical education at Penn State. Mr. Bezdek held a strong opinion about the playing time of baseball games. They were much too long, he argued.

One afternoon in May of that year, Mr. Bezdek instituted some new rules in a game between Penn State and Dickinson College. All through that game a batter was called out on two strikes, and got his walk on three balls. At the conclusion of the contest, Mr. Bezdek consulted his watch and remarked that the game had taken only an hour and twenty minutes, proving that his idea was sound. The big dumbbells who run the major leagues, however, paid no attention whatever to his discovery. Just as they pay no attention to a lady who's agin deliberate walks.

THE MATTER OF bearded baseball players was threshed out in New York's federal court in 1934. One of the nation's most famous ball teams for many years, of course, has been the House of David team, whose members conceal their emotions behind bushy beards. The management of this team went to court seeking an injunction against a certain Louis Murphy of Spring Valley, Illinois. Mr. Murphy had been traipsing around the country with a team of bearded ballplayers, cutting into the business and drawing power of the House of David club.

Judge John M. Woolsey read his opinion in court.

"From time immemorial," he said, "beards have been in the public domain. In respect of matters in that domain, all men have rights in common. Any man, therefore, if so minded, may —without being subject to challenge, legal or equitable—not only grow such a beard as he can but may purposely imitate another's facial shrubbery—even to the extent of following such topiary modification thereof as may have caught his fancy."

The House of David people were squirming by this time. It sure sounded as if the judge was against them.

"When," Judge Woolsey continued, "there is added to the wearing of beards by the defendant's baseball team the un-authorized wearing of uniforms bearing the words 'House of David' and that is accompanied by the booking of a team so equipped with the obvious intention of competing for gate receipts with the plaintiff's team, a cause of action on the defendant's part is established and it becomes clear beyond peradventure . . ."

And the injunction was granted.

THE OFFICIAL RULES say that a bat must be round, not over two and three fourths inches in diameter at its thickest part, and not more than forty-two inches in length. It must be made of hardwood entirely in one piece (this latter requirement would appear to mean that a player can't step up there carrying a bat with a hinge in it).

There have been some unusual bats, however, in the history of baseball.

Civilian employees of the United States Army, working in a Panamanian jungle in 1929, dug up a railroad tie that had been buried since 1850. Cut from lignum vitae wood, the tie had once been used on the railroad line built across the Isthmus in the time of the California gold rush. The workmen let the seventy-nine-year-old railroad tie lay around for a few days, unable to decide what they should do with it. Then someone got the happy idea of making a bat out of it and presenting it to Babe Ruth. The Babe received the bat in a presentation ceremony at the opening of the 1929 season.

SOMEWHERE in the charred ruins of the Baltimore Orioles' ball park, burned to the ground in 1944, was a lump of molten glass. It was all that remained of one of the many trophies accumulated by the Orioles down through the years. It dated back to 1894 when the Orioles, under the managerial genius of Ned Hanlon, won the championship in a series at Chicago. On their way home in triumph, the Orioles paused in Cumberland, Maryland, where a delegation of fans presented them with a beautiful glass bat, Cumberland being a glass-manufacturing center. The bat, etched with the inscription, "To Ned Hanlon and his Orioles —Champions of the World," was the one destroyed in the fire.

THE ARRESTED MAN'S NAME was Anthony Ferrara and he stood accused of driving an automobile at an excessive speed along a California highway.

"What business are you in?" asked the judge.

"I'm a baseball pitcher," said the prisoner.

The judge leaned forward and looked at him more closely.

"Oh, sure," he said, "you're Tony Ferrara from Merced." His Honor then reflected a moment. "Maybe you're lucky," he finally resumed, "and again maybe you're not. I'm going to give you a chance to escape punishment. Win the next game you pitch and you don't have to bother any more about this case. But if you lose it, we'll be sending out for you and you'll get a fine or even a jail sentence."

Tony was nervous a few days later when he went to the mound. He figured that if he lost just by a little bit, he'd be fined; but if he got massacred by the opposition, he'd go to jail. So he bore down—and pitched a shutout.

EDDIE JOOST'S SHIRT (as well as Eddie Joost) figured in a weird sequence of events during a game between the Red Sox and the Athletics at Boston one September day in 1948. In the fourth inning Ted Williams was on third. Bill Goodman slapped a grounder toward Joost at shortstop—an easy chance, so it appeared. The ball didn't exactly get away from the shortstop; in fact, it stayed quite close to him. Just as he reached down to scoop it into his glove, it took a hop, hit the heel of his mitt, and went into his sleeve. The ball must have had some sort of unusual spin on it, for it traveled up the sleeve, negotiated the bend at the elbow, continued its journey to the hairpin curve at the armpit, and dropped down into the waist of Eddie's shirt.

Ted Williams could have scored and eaten a sandwich before Joost finally got his hand on that ball. But Ted never got off third base. The antics of the shortstop, clawing first at his sleeve, then his armpit and, finally, jerking out shirttails as if he had suddenly become infested with rattlesnakes, convulsed Williams with laughter, and a man convulsed is a man incapable of doing much running. Ted just stood there on the bag and howled—along with everyone else in the park except Eddie Joost.

KISSING is a custom rarely encountered on the baseball field, though it is not unknown. Sometimes an exuberant manager, carried away by joyous emotion, will embrace one of his players and kiss him on the cheek for having driven in the winning run. Bob Hope, in his capacity as part owner of the Cleveland Indians, appeared on the field one day in 1947 when the Indians were about to take on the St. Louis Browns. Hope walked over to the Cleveland pitcher, Bob Feller, and gave him a loud kiss under the left ear for luck. Feller and the Indians lost the game.

Some ten years ago three players with the Greenville club in the Coastal League had a kissing agreement. Parties to the compact were Outfielder Charlie Scagg, Catcher Leslie McGarity, and Infielder Harry Jenkins.

Under the terms of their agreement, whenever one member of the trio hit a home run he was to be kissed by the other two. Leslie got only two homers all season and had to do most of the kissing. Scagg got twelve round-trippers and Jenkins hit sixteen. All the kissing was done on the cheek, though one report said that was a modification of the original understanding.

During this same period a pitcher named Jodie Phipps, with Utica in the Canadian-American League, had his own kissing routine. Each time he won a game, immediately after the last put-out, he would run in from the mound, get down on his knees and kiss home plate. Said it was lucky, and he must have been right, for he won twenty games that season.

DURING THE HITLER WAR the management of the Brooklyn Dodgers hit upon a device for helping the cause. The streets of Flatbush, at certain hours, were alive with kids loaded down with all kinds of scrap iron, trudging in the direction of Ebbets Field. The club collected many tons of the needed metal by offering free admission to the kids who brought all they could carry to the park.

Down in Wilmington, Delaware, in 1941, a similar stunt brought a vast improvement in the public health. Edward F. Glennon, business manager of the Wilmington team, knew that a lot of local citizens suffered under the scourge of hay fever. He announced that any kid who brought a bushel of ragweed roots to the park on July 9 would be admitted free.

Five tons of the troublesome roots were toted to the park on that one day. The ladies of the Garden Club heard about it and asked Mr. Glennon to do a rerun on it. So a second ragweed day was announced and the kids ranged over the town's vacant lots. They had done such a thorough job the first time that now they were able to dig up only three tons of the roots. Sneezing in Wilmington, to be sure, was radically reduced.

WILLIAM F. CAREY, once head of Madison Square Garden, was easily one of the most colorful individuals ever connected with the government of New York City. He served as Commissioner of Sanitation under Fiorello LaGuardia, and the things he did to better conditions for the fourteen thousand employees of the department will long be remembered.

The Sanitation Department had a baseball team, as did the Police and Fire departments. The police commissioner, Lewis J. Valentine, was proud and boastful of his department's team, and justifiably so. Each year there was a sort of World Series, usually held in Yankee Stadium, with the two competing teams splitting the proceeds, the money going into their respective welfare funds. Almost always the big game found the Police meeting the Fire Department, and almost always the Police won and took down the bigger share of the purse. Sanitation, having a miserable team, simply never got into the stadium game. Sanitation, in fact, didn't even have a welfare fund.

Police Commissioner Valentine was accustomed to ribbing Bill Carey unmercifully about Sanitation's ball team, and finally Carey resolved to do something about it. One day he called in a man named Farrell who knew baseball and asked him why it was that the Police Department team always won. Farrell explained that there were a number of former big-league ballplayers on the police team, and that made all the difference in the world. Well, said Carey, how do you go about getting big-league ballplayers to perform for these unimportant teams? Farrell explained that baseball was full of aging players looking toward their own future, eager for the security of steady jobs and the prospect of retirement on pensions. Well, said Bill Carey, could Farrell get him some ballplayers?

The whole operation was conducted in great secrecy. Carey interviewed and engaged eighteen men who had had experience in organized baseball. At this time the Sanitation Department had just acquired thirty new steel barges for hauling garbage. Carey went to the Civil Service Commission and asked for a new classification for men working on these barges. After long argument and negotiation, a new classification—scowman—was established. Candidates were required to have a knowledge of river boating plus actual experience on the river. Carey took his ballplayers and set up a sort of school in a Sanitation Department barn on the East River. He engaged a river expert to teach the men all about ropes and tides and currents and whistle toots. Inside that barn, hidden from the eyes of the world and especially from Commissioner Valentine, the ballplayers learned river boating. When they were ready for their civil-service tests, Carey sent each of them up the river to Rikers Island and back on the scows—so they could truthfully say that they had had actual experience on the river. All eighteen passed the tests. Quietly they began playing ball for the Sanitation team. And all this while Valentine continued ragging Carey about the miserable ball team he had.

Came the day when this rejuvenated Sanitation team met the Police for the first time. It had been Carey's intention to tell his boys to take it easy, fumble a few, maybe even let the cops win; he wanted to save the major assault for the big game at Yankee Stadium. Commissioner Valentine came over to Carey's box to administer a last-minute needling, and Carey decided to give his boys their heads. They smothered the Police team 17 to 3. Valentine was in a fury—never in his memory had the lowly Sanitation Department beaten his cops. But now Sanitation had a ball team, and they went on to win the big money for at least a half-dozen years in a row. And Sanitation got its welfare fund.

The Sanitation Department players, incidentally, were a sight to behold on the playing field. The various Sanitation slogans used on signs along the city streets were repeated in the lettering on the backs of the players' shirts. On the back of the catcher, for example, was the slogan: KEEP OUR CITY CLEAN. The first baseman was USE TRASH BASKETS. And the shortstop, a skillful man in a double play, wore the slogan: CURB YOUR DOG.

BACK IN JUNE of 1942, in the time of World War II, it had become customary for fans to throw back any ball that was batted into the stands. The Dodgers were playing the Cubs at Wrigley Field one afternoon when a Brooklyn batter fouled one into the stands back of first base. A young lady sitting in the fourth row got the ball and clutched it to her breast. After a reasonable wait, the public-address-system speaker spoke: "Will fans who get foul balls in the stands kindly throw them back on the field?"

The young lady stood up and, in the fashion of females, let go an overhand throw. The ball hit a man in the first row, catching him squarely in the back of the neck and fetching a howl of pain from him. The girl had speed but no control. Someone finally tossed the ball onto the field just as the loud-speakers boomed a second admonition: "Will fans who get foul balls in the stands kindly hold them until an usher comes to get them?"

IT'S A MARVELOUS THING to see the way a good outfielder plays the wall, reckoning precise angles and speeds and putting himself in the exact spot where the rebound will come to him. No outfielder, however, has ever done a better job of calculating angles than Charlie Schmidt—a catcher.

The Detroit Tigers were engaged in a contest one afternoon many years ago. George Mullin was pitching for Detroit, and Charlie Schmidt was catching. The opposition worked a runner around to third and at this point Schmidt called for time and walked out to the mound.

"George," he said, "I want you to throw a wild pitch."

"Who, me?" demanded Mullin. Never, in all his career, had he heard such a proposal.

"Look," said Charlie. "You see that spot on the wall back there where the paint's chipped a little? Take dead aim and throw hard and hit that spot. We'll get this guy on third."

He had to explain a little more carefully before Mullin got the idea. He was to throw a wild pitch deliberately, hitting the wall back of the plate. The ball would rebound at an angle which the catcher had calculated. Schmidt would be there to get it. The runner would try to score, but Mullin would race in to the plate. Schmidt would throw the ball to him, and he would tag the man out.

It worked perfectly.

OKLAHOMA is proud of the ballplayers the state has produced, especially in the pitching department. Among the contemporary pitchers in the big leagues who came out of the Sooner State are Alpha Brazle, Harry Brecheen, Joe Dobson, Bob Muncrief and Allie Reynolds. Yet not one of these men ever put on a performance to equal that of Paul Richards.

Back in July of 1928 the Topeka club came into Muskogee for a series of games with the local club. Soon after the contest got going the Topekans ran wild. The Muskogee manager, operating with a mound staff that was already crippled, found himself in a deep quandary. He simply ran out of pitchers, and he was pretty desperate until Paul Richards spoke up. Paul was the Muskogee shortstop, locally famous because of the fact that he could throw equally well with either hand. He volunteered to go in and pitch against the Topekans.

The third batter to face Paul was a fellow named Wilson, who was a switch-hitter. Up to that moment Richards had been pitching as a left-hander, so Wilson decided to bat right-handed. As soon as he took his position in the box, Richards switched his glove, somewhat clumsily, to his left hand and prepared to pitch with his right. Whereupon Wilson hopped over to the other side of the plate. Richards promptly converted himself into a lefty again, and Wilson, equal to the occasion, switched positions. This sort of maneuvering went on for a while, without a ball being thrown. It could have been a stalemate, but Richards finally decided on a course of action. He would pitch first with his right hand, then with his left hand, then back to right, and so on—regardless of where the batter was standing.

With the pitcher alternating from left to right, Wilson in turn hopped back and forth in the batter's box. The count ran to three balls and two strikes. Richards threw the next pitch with his left hand, Wilson stood on the right side of the plate and let it go by. It was a ball. He trotted on down to first, employing both his right leg and his left leg.

"OLD MAN SCROGMAN'S sure going to hell in a hurry," observed a citizen standing near the ball park in Terre Haute, Indiana, one afternoon about forty years ago. The remark was inspired by a runaway funeral. The cortege had been proceeding toward the cemetery, along a road that paralleled the right-field wall of the ball park. Inside, a game was in progress and a batted ball had landed just in front of the horses pulling the hearse. The ball scared the horses, hence the runaway.

This sort of thing happened on a number of occasions, and the people of Terre Haute began to complain. There was no other road to the cemetery—a funeral had to pass the ball park —and the high-minded citizens of the town demanded that something be done to prevent recurrences of these runaways. A departed one, they said, was entitled to a little dignity in his last ride.

The management of the ball park agreed, but didn't want to cancel ball games on account of funerals. Finally they arrived at a solution. They acquired a hand bell, of the type sometimes used by schoolteachers to signal the end of recess. Then they picked out a spot in the grandstand where a man could sit and command a view of the road. Thereafter, during every game, this fellow sat up there with his bell, his eye on the road. When he saw a funeral approaching, he rang the bell, the umpire called time, and the game stopped. The interruption continued until the funeral procession was out of range, whereupon the man clanged his bell again, and play was resumed.

JAY KIRKE was a first baseman and a character. There was the time a runner was taking a long lead off first when the pitcher fired the ball over to Jay. The runner made a slamming slide to get back. As the dust settled Jay glanced down and saw that his glove, with the ball in it, was jammed between the runner's foot and the base— clearly signifying the man was out. Yet the umpire had called him safe. Jay didn't move from his awkward position, but yelled at the umpire: "My God, you blind? Looka here! His foot ain't even touchin' th' bag!" The umpire had already seen it. "How about *you* lookin'," he yelled at Jay. "That's yer own foot, ya big dumb ox!" And so it was.

The best of the Jay Kirke stories concerns the big hit he didn't get at Chattanooga. Jay had been up in the big time until National League pitchers discovered that he was a sucker for a curve ball. He was constitutionally and congenitally unable to come within a foot of a curve. So he was sent down to Chattanooga where the celebrated Kid Elberfield was his manager.

The southern pitchers, of course, knew of Jay's weakness and they curve-balled him silly. During a game one afternoon Chattanooga got a runner on second. The next batter lined a single to the outfield and Jay, who was next up, was standing in front of the dugout awaiting his turn. The man on second was running, intent upon scoring on the single. The outfielder retrieved the ball and threw for the plate. It was a wild throw, however, and came straight at Jay Kirke. Instead of stepping aside, however, Jay cocked his bat and swung and knocked it clear to the fence. The umpire, goggle-eyed for a moment over this performance, ruled that the runner would have scored anyway, and that the hitter had to stay at first because of interference.

Jay now walked to the plate, the pitcher fed him curve balls, and he struck out. When he returned to the bench Kid Elberfield was waiting for him, spluttering with anger. What in the name of God, he demanded, had come over Jay to cause him to belt that outfield throw back into the field?

"Well, boss," said Jay sheepishly, "to tell you the truth, that's the first damn straight ball I've had come at me in months—the first ball I've seen that didn't have a curve on it. For the life of me I just couldn't keep from bustin' it one."

PULL UP A CHEER, son, and set, and I'll tell you about the time Harry Hardner got a five-base hit, as you might call it. Harry was a pitcher for the Walnut Street Cartage team, one of the best amateur outfits in the city of Milwaukee back around 1930. The Walnut Streeters were playing some other outfit and about halfway through the game Harry come up to bat. They didn't have no fences or nothing on this field, so's a man could really hit the long ball if he had a mind to. Harry had a mind to that day. He hauled off and whaled that ball halfway to Boone City, Ioway. The right fielder took off after it, and bets were being laid that he wouldn't be back till next Tuesday.

Old Harry did some running on them base paths. He come flying across home plate, happy as a goddam lark, just as the right fielder finally caught up with the ball and started returning it to the infield. But Harry got a big surprise when he crossed the plate. Some of his teammates were waiting for him, yelling like mad, telling him to get the hell down to first base fast as he could. Everybody in the park but Harry had noticed that he had failed to touch first on his way around the bases. He was tuckered, but he got in gear again, racing down the first-base line, and he made a long slide just before the ball thumped into the first baseman's glove.

The scorekeeper give Harry a single. Me, I call it a five-bagger.

THE BOX SCORE of an exhibition game between Cincinnati and Detroit in April of 1942 shows that Jimmy Bloodworth, leadoff man for the Tigers, got one hit in six times at bat. A box score is a cold and unemotional thing, and this one gave no hint of the fact that Bloodworth got his base knock with the assistance of the national anthem.

On the mound as the game was about to start stood the Cincinnati pitcher, Elmer Riddle. Bloodworth knocked the dirt from his spikes, hitched up his belt, and stepped into the batter's box. The catcher gave the sign, Riddle wound up and threw, and Bloodworth met the ball squarely. It was a hot shot back to the box. Riddle had just knocked it down when the opening bars of the "Star-Spangled Banner" came through the loud-speakers. The man in charge of O-say-can-you-see was a little tardy in putting on the record.

The ball, meanwhile, dribbled toward Second Baseman Lonnie Frey. Frey started to snatch it off the turf, then froze to attention, took off his cap and faced the flag. Bloodworth crossed first, then did likewise. When the last strains of the anthem died away, the scorekeeper penciled Jimmy in for a single, and the contest was resumed.

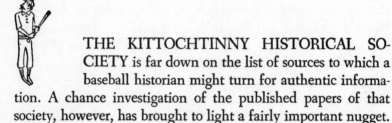

THE KITTOCHTINNY HISTORICAL SO-CIETY is far down on the list of sources to which a baseball historian might turn for authentic information. A chance investigation of the published papers of that society, however, has brought to light a fairly important nugget.

Up to now historians have been in agreement that the first game of baseball ever played at night under artificial lights was the one at Fort Wayne, Indiana, on June 2, 1883.

The Kittochtinny Historical Society is prepared to give Fort Wayne a forceful argument. In the society's archives is a paper describing a baseball game between George Pensinger's Paint Shop Nine and Captain Clay Henninger's team, played at Chambersburg, Pennsylvania, on the night of May 16, 1883.

These facts were contained in a paper read before the society in 1919 by H. A. Riddle. Thirty years later a baseball fan, Gerald G. McKelvey, of Waynesboro, happened on that old document and found in the text the following paragraph:

The first trial [of the lighting system] was made with a game of baseball on the show lot opposite the old passenger station, taking up that portion of the ground from Third Street to what was the Scheible Ponds. We had six lamps on the field, one 2,000-candlepower lamp hanging on a 25-foot pole in center field under a reflector on a piece of rope low enough to throw the light to the best advantage; also a lamp on a 16-foot pole at each base; one at home plate, set out of the way of the batter, and one back of the catcher. Distributed in this manner, the game was a success and was played as well as by daylight. Captain George Pensinger's Paint Shop Nine defeated Captain Clay Henninger's Nine of the town. The Franklin *Repository* has on file a paper giving a full account of the game, May 17, 1883.

With no regard for what Indiana and the city of Fort Wayne may think, Chambersburg has suddenly started pointing with pride. A local newspaperman, Frank Young of the Chambersburg *Public Opinion,* has set himself the job of gathering further information on that historic ball game, and in the end, no doubt, there'll be a marker or a monument on the spot where the first night game was played. Okay, boys—revise your books!

THE LATE FIORELLO LaGUARDIA, a gallant knight though small, proposed a piece of baseball legislation when he was a member of Congress back in 1925. Under his bill, which never got anywhere, a federal tax of 90 per cent would have been levied on all sales of baseball players whenever the sales price exceeded $5,000. The tax would have been nullified, however, if the player himself received the purchase price of his person.

Speaking for his plan, LaGuardia pointed out that baseball is the only business in which an individual fails to collect the profit which accrues through his own improved ability and the sale of that ability.

IN 1940 the Athletics and Indians were playing at Philadelphia and a high school band was present. When the moment came for the national anthem, nothing happened, so the Philadelphia pitcher threw one past Cleveland's leadoff man. As the ball thumped into the catcher's glove, the school kids got going on the anthem. When it was completed, Umpire Bill Summers ruled that the pre-anthem pitch didn't count, and the game was started all over again.

YEARS AGO Arch McDonald, the radio sportscaster who handles play-by-play accounts of games at Griffith Stadium in Washington, had a theme song which he played before and after his performance at the mike.

One afternoon the stage was set for the beginning of a game. The sportscaster spoke into his microphone: "And now, ladies and gentlemen, our national anthem!" The players on the field removed their caps and stood at attention. The mob in the stands did likewise. Deep silence reigned in the park. Then from the loud-speakers came the raucous strains of "Oh, They Cut Down the Old Pine Tree!" A bit later they cut down the old radio engineer who had put the wrong record on the turntable.

CEDAR RAPIDS was playing Kewanee one afternoon, and by the middle of the game Cedar Rapids was leading 16 to 1. The Kewanee boys were testy about it, and remarks were being passed. Suddenly the batter at the plate knocked the catcher down. In a trice (.08 of a second) fist fighting was in progress all over the field, and heavily muscled spectators were coming out of the stands to get in on the bloodletting. Suddenly all fighting stopped. The public-address-system jockey had put the "Star-Spangled Banner" on.

WHEN UMPIRES get together for shop talk, there is one remark that is sure to be made if Al Mutart is present. "You guys can talk all you want to," Al will say, "but I'm the only umpire ever had a *crutch* thrown at me."

The crutch was thrown by Manager Bill Sweeney of the Portland club during a game with Hollywood in 1949. Sweeney was on the bench with a lame foot, his crutch at his side, when Mutart made a decision that sent him into a conniption. He screamed, and then threw the crutch, but it was a bad throw and fell short of its mark. The fine imposed was $50.

THE TROUBLE with the people of North Carolina is that they are simply too dern friendly and obliging to us Yankees. A fantastic baseball story appears in the pages of the Raleigh *News and Observer*. Mr. Bill Sharpe, who is in favor of electricity in North Carolina, remembers that some people named Smith are collecting baseball stories, clips the *News and Observer* piece, and sends it to us. At the same time some other congenial Tar Heel clips it and sends it to the wrong Smith—Mr. Red Smith of the New York *Herald Tribune*. And Mr. Red Smith prints it in his column, doggone his Green Bay hide, and now we'll be accused of larceny. Nevertheless, the story of the ball game in the little town of Seven Paths, North Carolina, ought to be chiseled in stone, word for word, and preserved at Cooperstown. Here is the way it appeared in the Raleigh paper:

> Mrs. Henry Denton of Route 2, Middlesex, sends in an old clipping which originally appeared in the *News and Observer*. It concerns a baseball game between Seven Paths and Gold Valley in July, 1890. The Gold Valley boys left home at noon and walked eight miles, barefooted, to the game. The game started at 1:30 and the battle raged for six and a half hours . . . The final score? 240 to 169 . . . To quote the story:
>
> "Ben Gay was on the mound for Seven Paths and was in great form, allowing only 102 hits. But he did not receive good backing from his teammates. Onnie Whitley did the hurling for Gold Valley and allowed only 93 hits and got good support from his mates.
>
> "Several feature plays were made by members of both teams, but T. Denton, better known as Slim Denton (for he wore pants 26 inches in the waist and 51 inches long), made

a spectacular catch in center field when he climbed a tree to rob Ben Wood of a hit to the woods.

"Peter Denton, who held down second base for Gold Valley, was great in the pinches but otherwise he had 63 errors to his credit. Crad Brantley made the greatest hitting average, getting 47 hits out of 77 times at bat.

"Umpire Nate Strickland's decisions were fair and above reproach. If a batter struck at a ball that didn't go squarely over the plate, he called it a ball and said he'd be confounded if he'd call anything like that a strike; but that brought no protest from the opposing team.

"Tinker Denton came near causing a sensation when he hit a double home run, making two trips around the circuit. Umpire Strickland said 'twas fair.

"Thus the game went for the whole afternoon. Umpire Strickland said that only darkness could halt such a wonderful game, which he said was the finest he had ever seen. Nearly 300 people attended."

A COUPLE OF YEARS after George McBride joined the Washington club around 1910 he ran into a stretch of games during which he booted a lot of balls that came his way at shortstop. Temperate criticism of his clumsiness appeared in the sports pages, and intemperate remarks were directed at him by the fans, but it remained for one spectator at the Washington park to deliver an active rebuke.

Detroit and Washington were just changing places between innings and McBride was in the act of tossing his glove onto the grass when this critic, drunk as a billy goat, broke out of the grandstand and ran on the field. He went straight to shortstop, picked up McBride's glove, put it on, spit in the center of it, pounded the spit in with his fist, faced the plate, crouched slightly, and said: "Watch how *I* do it, McBride, you big ninny!" The cops grabbed him and threw him about three blocks, putting stuff on him so he dropped sharply, and from that moment on Shortstop McBride's fielding slump was ended.

Some years later at Wrigley Field in Chicago another drunk came over the barrier, his bottle in his hand, and made for second base. A policeman chased after him. Midway between first and second the two men met. The drunk thrust the bottle at the cop and the cop, momentarily confused, took it. The drunk then whipped off his coat and essayed a spectacular demonstration of how a man should slide into second. The policeman, meanwhile, stood like a statue, holding the whisky bottle away from his body as if it were an adder. The drunk got up, dusted himself off, retrieved his coat and put it on, took the bottle from the cop and scampered off, disappearing into the stands before the officer could recover from the shock of it all.

In the time of these happenings such unscheduled performances by fans were rare. During the last year or so there have been many instances of spectators, drunk and sober, racing onto the field during play. The ball-park cops have been unable to figure out a way to put a stop to the practice. We'd suggest elephant guns. Some sports writers have said flatly that television is responsible—that the exhibitionistic fans want to perform on TV. That could be, but we have a more reasonable explanation: human beings are growing steadily goofier with each passing year.

OUR VICE-PRESIDENT in charge of digging has come into possession of an interesting book published in 1888 by A. J. Reach & Co. The title follows:

HYGIENE

—FOR—

BASE BALL PLAYERS

—BEING A—

*Brief Consideration of the Body as a Mechanism;
The Art and Science of Curve Pitching; A
Discussion of the Causes and Treatment
of the Disabilities of Players;
With a Few Practical Hints
To Club Managers.*

The author is A. H. P. Leuf, M.D., of Philadelphia, who identifies himself in the text as a former baseball player. A large portion of the book is given over to a description of the human skeleton and the multitude of muscles which it carries around; the rest of the text is a long harangue in favor of clean living. Sounds quite dull—yet this textbook for ballplayers, active in the Year of the Big Blizzard, has its interesting points.

Dr. Leuf shows, for example, that the principal muscles employed by a pitcher in throwing a curve ball are the shoulder extensors, forearm flexors, supinators, deltoid, teres major, biceps, brachialis anticus, pectoralis major, serratus magnus, and latissimus dorsi. It hardly seems worth it—a man might as well stick to his high hard one.

The doctor talks a good deal about ballplayers chinning themselves—the principal form of exercise in those days, along with playing tug of war. He appears to be in favor of anger on the diamond, declaring that angry ballplayers generally play better than placid ones. He adds, however: "Do not eat while laboring under excitement of any kind, whether it be of joy, sorrow, or anger, for all alike affect the heart so as to retard or prevent digestion." A bad rule, we feel. There are quite a few ballplayers nowadays who, if they followed that regulation, would surely starve to death.

Dr. Leuf says ballplayers should sleep on horsehair mattresses to keep from getting one side of their heads hot; he also advises them never to sleep with the mouth open. He goes all out against drinking alcoholic beverages of any kind, declaring flatly that it will take anywhere from twenty to thirty years off a man's life even if done in moderation. He ranks drunkards with lunatics, imbeciles, epileptics, and idiots and then comes through in the clutch with his clincher: "If men who are desirous of having sons who will grow up good, bright and strong healthy men, they must give up drink, for bad qualities and defects are not only inherited, but are, as a rule, intensified by heredity."

Preaching against the use of tobacco by ballplayers, the doctor says: "Note, for instance, the repose and extreme satisfaction with which a previously worried individual will sit down to a smoke, or how indifferently the tobacco chewer, as a rule, regards matters around him, as compared with himself when not chewing or when he totally abstains from the use of this fatal drug. Why look down upon an opium smoking celestial if you are a tobacco smoker yourself? . . . Because of tobacco's sedative or depressing effect upon the mind, it inclines one to avoid as much exertion as possible, in other words, it tends to laziness."

He declares that the same stuff a ballplayer wads into his mouth when applied as a poultice to parts of the body often make patients "deathly sick." And he adds: "It is a fact that many ballplayers today bat poorly because of their having tobacco eyes."

Dr. Leuf hits his peak when, in his advice to club managers, he discusses the matter of personal cleanliness on the part of ballplayers.

"Compel every man," he writes, "to wash or rinse his feet in a bucket of water after each game.

"Insist upon every man taking a bath at least once a week under penalty of a fine, and make him do it under your eyes at the hotel or on the club grounds.

"Strictly enforce a rule requiring all players to have their uniforms washed once a week and also make them dry their uniforms after each game. Never permit the unhealthy and foul and disgusting custom of leaving damp uniforms and stockings on the floor, or on a chair, or in the bottom of a closet."

The doctor specifies, when he speaks of bathing, the use of a tub. Shower baths, he says, are dangerous and useless.

"Shower baths," he announces, "do no good but a great deal of harm. It is seldom safe to use one except under the direction of a competent physician."

And further than that, the book says, every ballplayer should be in bed and asleep by ten o'clock, and up at six, and feather beds are no good.

Anybody got a chaw of terbaccer? We ain't ballplayers.

 MIKE GONZALES was a catcher for the Cubs in 1926 and at the end of the season got a team together and headed for Mexico for some winter ball playing. The venture was a success and the Americans came back with their wallets considerably fattened.

Came the end of the 1927 season and Gonzales decided to try

it again. He took his team first to a Mexican town not far over the border. The Americans played several games and heard a lot of talk about a revolution that was brewing. They weren't disturbed about it. The man who was to pay them off for their work in this particular town told them he'd see them in Mexico City with the cash.

In the Mexican capital the paymaster was just calling on Gonzales and his players when a squad of soldiers arrived, grabbed the Mexican, marched him out to a convenient wall, and shot him dead. The soldiers turned around now to inform the *Americanos* that this paymaster dog had been mixed up with the revolutionists. But the *Americanos* were not there any longer. With Mike Gonzales in the lead, they had taken their departure in haste, and they didn't stop traveling until they were across the border.

WITHOUT CEREMONY, the Yankees unveiled a new left-handed pitcher at Detroit one afternoon in 1931. His name was Vernon Gomez. Just before the contest Bob Shawkey, the New York manager, indulged in a skull session with his young pitcher. They studied the list of Detroit batsmen and Shawkey outlined the strategy to be used against each of them. "Now this one," he said, "this Gehringer —I want you to be extra careful with him. Don't ever give him a fat one or he'll bust up the game for you."

The Yankees went down in order in their half of the first and then Gomez went to the mound. He retired the first two Detroiters; then the third man up powdered the ball out of the park. Gomez got the next batter to foul out and returned to the Yankee bench. He was feeling that he hadn't done *too* bad, all things considered, yet here was Manager Shawkey glaring at him as if he had just walked nine straight batters.

"Skipper," said Gomez, "it was this way. I kinda slipped and stumbled on a bad piece of ground the crazy groundkeepers hadn't smoothed down, and just about then some jerk in the stands shone a mirror in my eyes, and they musta put starch in my uniform because the shirt gave a yank across the back and held my arm back, and that ball has got something wrong with it—they musta brought it up from the minors, it's so lopsided, and—— But listen, Skipper. I know how to get that Gehringer guy. I'll fix *him* when he comes up."

"He's already come up," growled Shawkey. "He hit that homer."

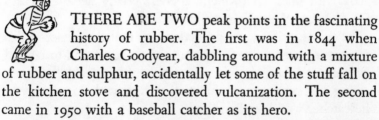 THERE ARE TWO peak points in the fascinating history of rubber. The first was in 1844 when Charles Goodyear, dabbling around with a mixture of rubber and sulphur, accidentally let some of the stuff fall on the kitchen stove and discovered vulcanization. The second came in 1950 with a baseball catcher as its hero.

Early in the season of 1950 a sports writer was loafing around the Braves' bench up in Boston, picking up chitchat before the start of the day's game. Noticing a catcher's mitt alongside of him, the newspaperman casually picked it up and tried it on. His hand encountered something soft and squdgy and nice. It is unlikely that he thought it was what it was supposed to represent. What on earth would a woman's—well, what would a thing like that be doing in a catcher's mitt? Anyway, he dragged it out and his eyes popped. It was a falsie, one of the larger achievements of our flowering civilization. Fashioned of soft sponge rubber, it was designed to fit over one half the chest of

a lady with small endowment, thereby giving her the appear
ance of Marie Wilson after a heavy meal.

The sports writer's first deduction was that the owner of this
mitt was in love, and was carrying the thing around to remind
him constantly of his fair one. He couldn't resist, however,
locating the catcher and challenging him with his discovery.
The catcher wasn't embarrassed.

"Best thing I've ever found to use in my mitt," he said.
"Takes up the shock of a hard pitch better'n shammy leather,
or any other kinda rubber, and fits real nice to the hand. Quite
a few catchers using them now."

OFFICIALS of the Southeastern League went into a huddle back in 1939 seeking some means of minimizing the amount of time taken up during ball games with argument and quarreling. They finally emerged with a new regulation, which provided that any player who yapped at an umpire for more than two minutes would automatically be banished from the game.

Efforts to enforce the new rule brought on greater delays than had been the case before it was invoked.

There was the time, for instance, when Billy Bancroft, manager of the Selma club, got himself kicked out of a game for *deliberately* continuing an argument with an umpire for longer than two minutes.

Five minutes earlier there had been another rhubarb. Manager Bancroft, with a watch in his hand, had yammered at the umpire for precisely a minute and a half, then he had turned and walked off the field. Now, on a close play at second base, he let his jaw wag furiously for two full minutes, and then he kept wagging it, and the umpire informed him that he had violated the rule.

"The hell I have," said Bancroft. "I got a half minute credit coming to me on that last argument. I get two and a half minutes this time."

This interpretation of the rules was knocked down by the umpire, though there were some who said Billy Bancroft was right—he ought to be allowed to store up time and use it all in one bunch.

In all events, the rule wasn't enforced for long—it caused too much loss of time through argument.

CAPTAIN ISRAEL BAKER, a lobster fisherman of Orrs Island, Maine, arrived at the age of sixty-five in 1940 without ever having seen a major-league baseball game. From his boyhood on he had been a follower of big-league ball but he just never had been able to manage getting to a game. Now he had saved up enough for a junket "up" to Boston where, for the first time, he would see in the flesh his favorite of favorites—Jimmy Foxx.

The captain bought his way into the ball park, toting a crate containing a dozen fine Maine lobsters. He argued his way down to the field boxes and succeeded in calling Foxx over. Then he told Foxx his story—how he admired him above all other ballplayers, and how this was the first time he'd ever had a chance to see Jimmy play.

"So," said Captain Baker, "I brought these fine lobsters along, and if you'll do me the favor of hitting a home run, you can have every dad-blame one of them. If you don't hit a home run, then you got to split 'em up with Ted Williams."

The game got tied up and went into extra innings and then in the last of the eleventh Jimmy Foxx, with lobsters on his mind, teed off and got his homer.

The good captain returned to Maine happy. Today at seventy-five he is still a fisherman, but he informs us, by government courier, that he spends a good deal of time looking at a newfangled machine he recently bought—a television set. He looks at it only when it has baseball on it.

FROM THE FILES of the United States Civil
Service Commission in Washington we have an
application for government employment dated in
June of 1949. The applicant described himself as a hard working umpire with three years of experience at his job. He was
seeking a job as a personnel officer in the government, and he
set out to prove that his work as an umpire qualified him for
such a position.

"As an umpire," he wrote, "I am in complete charge of the
game and all participating personnel.

"I must be able to formulate instantaneous decisions regarding various plays as to whether the players are 'out' or 'safe.'

"I must be thoroughly familiar with all rules of the game and be able to apply them at the proper time and to the proper play.

"I must be able to handle people in as much as arguments sometimes arise regarding my decision on a play, and I must be able to restore order and quiet the group so play can resume. I must be able to control crowds of spectators, keep them from interfering with the game or players.

"The players are entirely dependent upon me for the proper direction of the game from the start to the finish."

The commission turned him down. Figured, possibly, that he had bum eyes.

A PRESS ASSOCIATION carried a home-run story out of Albany, New York, one day in 1940. It involved a clothing store across the street from the local ball yard. A clerk was alone in the store when a home-run ball crashed through the window. The clerk was not overly disturbed—that window had been shattered quite a few times in the past. But this time the ball came through the glass, hit the keys of the cash register and rang up a sale of $2.34. This left the clerk in a quandary, for he would have to explain away the shortage of $2.34 on the day's sales, and it would be difficult to convince his boss that a home run was responsible.

The press-association man who wrote and sent out that item was a liar by the clock.

There is, however, a related story that is authentic, and by coincidence it involved a ballplayer from Albany—fellow named George Savino. He started the 1936 season with Albany, did good, and was moved up to Baltimore in the International League. The first time he came to bat for the Orioles he walloped a home run.

Across the street from the park on that Sunday afternoon a lady had just finished putting a magnificent family dinner on the table. Savino's home-run ball came through the window, hit squarely in the middle of the table, and in no time at all there was gravy on the ceiling, celery and olives scattered clean to the kitchen, and the chicken looked as if it had been carved with a ball-peen hammer.

The housewife slapped on her hat, marched over to the ball park, told her story with exclamation points, and was liberally reimbursed by the management.

THE SPANISH LANGUAGE has been a factor in major-league ball games on several occasions. Down at Griffith Stadium in Washington one afternoon Roberto Ortiz, Senators' outfielder, got a two-base hit off a Cleveland pitcher. Roberto stood down at second and studied the signaling system of the Cleveland catcher. The next two batters were retired after some effort and by then Roberto had the signals figured out.

Now a fellow Cuban came to the plate in the person of the Washington pitcher, Conrado Marrero. Down at second Ortiz shouted at him: *"Te digo lo que va a tirar!"* Meaning, "I'll tell you what this bum's gonna throw!"

The catcher flashed his sign to the pitcher and Ortiz now yelled: *"Te va a dar la rápida!"* Meaning, "This-a fonnee man, he'sa gonna throw you fasta ball!" And be dad-blamed if he didn't! He threw a fasta ball, and Marrero whopped it for a single, and Ortiz scored.

Back in 1942 Salvador Hernandez, catcher for the Chicago Cubs, was always happy when Hiram Bithorn was his pitcher, for Hi knew Spanish and the two men did all their signaling aloud, in Spanish.

One afternoon the two señors were mowing down the New York Giants when trouble developed. In the seventh inning New York got two men on base and Hernandez, in Spanish, called for a curve ball. The batter smacked it for a double. The next two batters also appeared to know what pitches were ordered, for they got hits. Hi and Sal surveyed the situation uneasily and then got the answer. They spotted Adolfo Luque, Giant coach, who was conversant with Spanish. He had posted himself so that he could hear the catcher's signal and then quickly flash it to the batter. From that moment on the linguistic system of signaling was abandoned, and Hi and Sal went back to the old-fashioned use of fingers.

CHARLIE GRIMM has ample reason to remember the date of August 2, 1932. He remembers the day and he remembers the night. On that day he was named manager of the Chicago Cubs, succeeding Rogers Hornsby. A big day for him and a busy one, and he was late getting to his hotel room, which he shared with one of his star players.

During the night Charlie was awakened by movement in the room. He snapped on the light and saw his roommate engaged in a strange sort of pantomime. The ballplayer was on his knees in the middle of his bed. He was bending forward and, with great grunts and groans and whinnies, appeared to be pretending that he was trying to pull a stump out of the ground.

Charlie hopped out of bed and went over and woke the man up.

"You wrasslin' with a boa constrictor in your sleep or something?" demanded Charlie.

"No," said the ballplayer, "it was worsen that. I was dreamin'

I was on a farm that belongs to one of my kinfolks, and he had fell down the well and I had aholt of the rope and was tryin' to pull him out. Sure glad you woken me up. It was turrible!"

"It sure was," said Charlie, making a mental note to do some shifting around of room assignments the next day.

THE AUTHORS of this book make no claim to having affected the play of any game of baseball, yet there was an incident . . .

Our previous book, *Low and Inside*, contained a story about a variation of the hidden-ball trick; the base runner was caught off first after the first baseman had appeared to return the ball to the pitcher when, in fact, he had thrown a potato back to the mound.

A few weeks after that book appeared, the following story came out of Little Rock, Arkansas, by *AP* wire:

> With a runner on third in a City League game yesterday, the defensive catcher pulled a potato out of his pocket and threw it to third. The third baseman fumbled it and the runner broke for home. He was tagged by the catcher, who was holding the ball all the time.
>
> The plate umpire was confused, too, for a while. He called the runner out, then reversed the decision, allowing the runner to score.

The potato incident appeared in a Washington newspaper and caught the eye of Rear Admiral D. V. Gallery, who promptly sat down and wrote a letter to the paper's sports editor. Said he:

The umpire was obviously wrong in ruling the unobservant athlete safe. The runner was OUT.

There is not a single word in the baseball rule book about potatoes or any other groceries.

I predict a bright future in the big leagues for the wily catcher involved in this incident.

I also suggest that in order to prevent further waste of food and bewilderment of base runners who can't tell a baseball from a rutabaga, the big leagues at their next annual meeting should adopt the following rule:

"Base runners shall be entitled to advance one base, without liability of being put out, whenever the team in field puts in play any vegetable or fruit smaller than a watermelon."

WHEN JIMMY DYKES was managing the White Sox he had his troubles with a certain player who was known as "Clean Pants" because he wouldn't slide into a base unless somebody put a gun to his head.

Manager Dykes jawed him and jawed him, and still Clean Pants refused to slide. One afternoon the stand-up ballplayer was tagged out at home when he would have been safe had he slood. Dykes promptly slapped a ten-day suspension on him.

Three or four days later a club official came to Dykes and said he believed Clean Pants had learned his lesson and should be reinstated in the line-up.

"What makes you think so?" Dykes demanded.

"Well," said the informant, "I was out at Fairmount yesterday watching the horses run, and there was Clean Pants, on the rail, watching the third race. The horses came down the stretch in a close finish, and the horse Clean Pants was betting on was staying up there neck and neck with another horse.

Clean Pants was screaming his head off at his horse, and as the two leaders came down within a dozen yards of the finish line, he let go a yell that everybody in the park heard. 'Slide, you bum!' he yelled, 'SLIDE!' "

THERE WAS A DAY in 1912 when Casey Stengel, soon after he had joined the Brooklyn Dodgers, was not permitted in the dugout during an entire game. He was compelled to sit on the ground a few yards off to one side of the dugout. The reason for this expulsion, to be frank, was that Casey stunk.

The Dodgers had gone over to play an exhibition game in New Jersey and there were some extracurricular activities before play began. Among these events was a contest in which the ballplayers tried to catch a greased pig. Most of the players didn't have their heart in it but Casey gave it the old college try, for two reasons. First, he wanted the fifty-dollar prize that went to the winner, and second, he wanted to demonstrate to his new employers that he was a man who could hustle. So he went after that pig as if his life depended on it, and finally brought it down and wrapped himself around it and stayed there until the judges decreed him the winner.

Casey was so happy over his success that he, personally, didn't seem to notice anything wrong with himself. Any man who clamps onto a pig and wrestles it to the ground, even an ungreased pig, is not going to smell good. But Casey had all over him a combination of ordinary pig smell *plus* the smell of a particularly offensive brand of axle grease.

He got no congratulations, however, when he returned to the bench; all he got was "Peee-yew!" and much nose holding, and exile to a spot some distance from the dugout.

ONE EVENING many years ago John McGraw sat alone in a hotel dining room and contemplated the steak that the waiter had just put before him. It was one of the prettiest steaks ever seen, sizzling and juicy and as thick as an unabridged dictionary. McGraw looked at it lovingly, and surely his thoughts at that moment were far from the problem of Jack Scott.

All this took place at the Giant spring training camp. Jack Scott had come into camp a couple of weeks earlier, but he had refused to sign his contract. He demanded more money than had been offered him and he was holding firm. In the last few days Jack's supply of cash had dwindled and now he was behind in his room rent and, as for fodder, he was subsisting on little more than an occasional sandwich. Hungry as he was, he still refused to surrender on that contract.

So we have McGraw picking up his knife and fork. The Giant manager didn't even notice Jack Scott. One of the dining-room windows gave on the street and Scott, passing by, happened to glance in and see that steak. He pressed up close to the window and stared at it as McGraw dug in. He stared for a full minute, then turned and hurried into the hotel.

"Mr. McGraw," he panted, "let me sit down here and eat a steak like that and I'll sign at any figure you say."

Said McGraw: "Have a chair."

IN THE LATER MONTHS of World War II a unit of American troops, moving across the French countryside, stumbled on a young woman whose behavior aroused their suspicions. She was taken before a military intelligence officer, suspected of being a German spy. Under questioning she identified herself as Virginia von Lampe, and denied with vigor that she was a spy. She had lived in the United States for years, she said, making her home in Yonkers, New York. The questioning went along and she was having difficulty establishing her innocence, and then baseball saved her. The intelligence officer was trying to knock down her story of residence in America, and suddenly he threw a trick question at her: In baseball, he asked, what does the expression "feller" mean? She said she supposed it meant Bob Feller of the Cleveland Indians. He followed this with a long series of questions about baseball and baseball players, and the young woman knew all the answers—she appeared to know baseball better than Daniel M. Daniel M. Daniel. And from this beginning she was soon able to convince the intelligence man that she was no more a spy than he was.

VAUGHN HAZEN, a young man affiliated with the Columbus team of the American Association, got into only nine games during the 1944 season. Vaughn was used as a pinch hitter and officially was charged with only five times at bat that year. The book shows he got three hits in five times up, and one of those hits concerns us here. He got it by twice beating the throw to first.

With two men on base, the young man was sent in as a pinch hitter against Milwaukee. He banged a ground ball down to second and the Milwaukee infielder threw to first. Vaughn beat the throw for an infield single, but he misinterpreted the umpire's gesture and thought he had been called out. He started walking slowly back to the dugout and the first baseman returned the ball to Earl Caldwell, the Milwaukee pitcher.

As young Hazen neared the dugout he suddenly became conscious of frenzied yelling on the part of his teammates. They were telling him he had been safe, to get back to first base in a hurry, that the ball was still in play. He whirled and raced back toward the bag. Meanwhile Pitcher Caldwell, himself somewhat confused, was standing on the mound, facing away from first, the ball in his hand. Now *his* teammates started screaming. He woke up to what was going on, turned and fired the ball to first. Hazen slid into the bag, from a most unusual angle, coming at it from the direction of the dugout, and for the second time beat the throw.

That Columbus incident calls to mind one of the capers of the great Bobo Newsom along toward the close of his pitching career. He was at bat one afternoon for the Dodgers and dribbled the ball back to the box. The opposing pitcher picked it up and Bobo, who was making no pretense of running it out, stopped about eight steps down the first-base line, turned and walked back to the dugout. The pitcher watched him, still holding the ball, then turned his attention to the plate, where the next batter had taken his place.

Back in the dugout, Bobo went to the water cooler, took a long drink, and then suddenly he became a ball of fire. He came out of the dugout like a daft elephant, charging toward first base. The screams of the opposition players awakened the pitcher, who wasn't aware of what was happening. He threw to first just an instant before Bobo got there and the crowd roared its approval of a great try.

AROUND 1940 a young goon was picked up in Philadelphia as a suspect in a robbery case. "I couldn'ta done it," he argued, "because I was out at

Shibe Park." The assistant district attorney wanted to know what he had been doing at Shibe Park. Watchin' a ball game. Who was playing? The Athletics and the Yanks. Who won? The suspect knew the answer. But now the prosecutor, who had been at the game himself, began asking for details of the game, and the suspect tried to bluff it out, but he had things all wrong and, in the end, was convicted of the crime.

OLD-TIMERS will remember the name of Jakie Atz, a major-league star back yonder. His real name was John Jacob Zimmerman. When he was in the bush leagues he played under the name of Zimmerman. For a while he was with a club that sometimes had trouble meeting its pay roll. The players were required to line up at the pay window in alphabetical order; occasionally the money ran out before the man at the end of the line reached the window, and the man at the end of the line was always Zimmerman. So, the next time he shifted to another club, he became Jakie Atz, and he remained Jakie Atz through the rest of his career.

AN UMPIRE working in the American Association in the 1930s called himself O'Brien, and appeared in the box scores under that name. His real name, however, was Harold Schieffelbein. The most satisfactory explanation of why he changed it concerns his sympathetic feeling toward spectators. He realized it was difficult for an enraged fan to howl: "Why, Schieffelbein, you grave-robbin', mother-floggin' son-of-a-buck, you oughta be stood up and shot!"

It was much easier for the fan to say such things when the name was O'Brien.

BILL KLEM remembers the day he was umpiring a Pittsburgh game back in 1913 when a brand-new rookie outfielder was sent up to the plate as a pinch-hitter. As the youngster arrived at the dish, bat in hand, Umpire Klem said to him: "What's your name?"

The pinch-hitter turned and said to Klem: "Boo."

Klem had heard many a boo from the grandstand in his time, but this one was a boo he could handle.

"Listen, you fresh busher," he growled, "you're out of the game before you're even in it! Beat it!"

It took a little time to get it straightened out, but the kid did get to bat after he convinced Klem that his true name was Everett L. Booe.

PREACHER ROE was never a preacher, nor did he ever aspire to the ministry. When he was an infant, lying in his Arkansas crib, he would flap his arms wildly and yammer unintelligible gibberish at the top of his tiny voice.

One day a neighbor woman happened in, heard the racket, took a long look at the baby, and said:

"Derned if he don't act jist like a preacher!"

Thus he became "Little Preacher" and later on "Preacher" and very seldom "Elwin."

THE VILLAGE of Dobbs Ferry is a peaceful community perched on the east bank of the Hudson River. It played a small part in the Revolutionary War, was the home of the agnostic Bob Ingersoll, and achieved passing fame in 1929 as the battleground of the great war between Baseball and Golf.

In 1924 Edwin Gould had given the village a $20,000 tract of land for a playground. The Gould playground adjoined the golf course of the Ardsley Club, and members of the club objected to its occasional use by grown men playing baseball. Matters reached a head during the Fourth of July week in 1929.

The annual baseball game for the village championship had been scheduled for the playground on July Fourth, between the Dobbs Ferry Athletic Association and Murphy's All Stars. The Ardsley Club went to court and got an injunction forbidding the ball game.

Most of the townspeople immediately raised a holler against the "swells" of the Ardsley Club. The caddies, mostly village boys, got together and talked plans for a strike against the golfers. One of the Dobbs Ferry trustees, a Mr. Polemus, said the injunction was part of a plot to dethrone the national game of baseball from its historic position and substitute the foreign importation of cow-pasture pool. "They are trying to make golf the national game," he declared.

Village Counsel Ellery Albee obtained a postponement of hearings on the injunction to July 12 and then, on Independence Day, the two ball teams played their game at the Gould playground. Over on the golf course the indignant Ardsley clubbers were, for the most part, carrying their own bags.

The whole village turned out, of course, for the ball game and there were many cars parked in the vicinity, especially along Belden Avenue. This thoroughfare crossed the golf links between the tee and the green on the fifth hole. Golfers had to play across the roadway, which was now thickly populated with parked cars.

During the afternoon a Mrs. J. S. Langthorn drove a ball into the rough near the roadway and found it nestled in the grass a few yards in front of a parked car. She issued a loud demand that the car be moved so she could play out. A small crowd gathered, including Michael Giuliano, owner of the car. He refused to move the car. Whereupon Mrs. Langthorn hauled out her No. 2 iron, took careful aim, and drove the ball crashing through the windshield of Mr. Giuliano's automobile.

Feeling was running pretty high now, and a free-for-all was averted only by the arrival of Dobbs Ferry Police Chief Costello. Mr. Giuliano demanded the arrest of Mrs. Langthorn, charging her with malicious mischief, and she was taken into town and placed under bail bond. Meanwhile the ball game proceeded to its conclusion.

The Baseball-Golf War petered out after that. Everybody cooled off, and all court actions were adjudicated in a sportsmanlike atmosphere and it was agreed, all around, that there is room for both games in the United States.

GEORGE C. JACKSON was an outfielder with the Boston Braves in 1911, staying on until the end of the 1913 season. During those three years George had a habit of misjudging fly balls more than is customary among good outfielders. But he had an alibi. He was forever complaining to the manager that ocean wind caused him trouble. He pointed out that most of his errors were committed in home games—right in Boston—where the strong breezes off the ocean had a tendency to blow the ball out of his reach.

"Seems funny," the manager told him, "that none of the other boys got any complaint to make on account of the ocean breeze."

George Jackson insisted, however, that the winds off the sea were his undoing, and along toward the end of the 1913 season he came up with a proposal. He said he wanted to be traded to St. Louis or Cincinnati, where he'd do most of his playing out of range of the ocean breeze. The management, grown tired of his quarrel with the Atlantic, obliged him after a fashion—they dropped him clear out of the league.

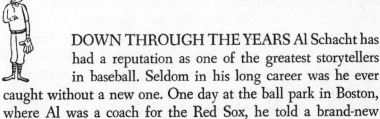 DOWN THROUGH THE YEARS Al Schacht has had a reputation as one of the greatest storytellers in baseball. Seldom in his long career was he ever caught without a new one. One day at the ball park in Boston, where Al was a coach for the Red Sox, he told a brand-new yarn to Moe Berg, the intellectual catcher, and Moe laughed fit to kill, and Al figured that was a sign that his latest story was a dinger.

That evening Al came down from his room to the hotel lobby and saw Moe Berg and several other ballplayers in a huddle. As he came up to the group, Berg said, "Hey, Al, tell the boys that one you told me at the park this afternoon."

It was a fairly long story but Al started on it eagerly. He was about halfway through, building suspense, when one of the players quietly turned his back and walked away. Then another did the same, and another—until Al was standing there with his mouth open and no audience whatever.

He was pretty upset—he'd never had anybody walk out on one of his stories before. He thought that maybe he was losing his talent. Then Moe Berg came up and took him off the hook; Moe had prearranged the whole maneuver as a gag.

BACK IN 1882 the bark *Trinity* was wrecked and the crew made it ashore on an island. Apparently this was an island without the usual complement of full-bosomed native girls, for the hairy-chested New England salts had difficulty figuring out what they could do with all the time on their hands. Then someone suggested baseball.

They organized two teams and laid out a diamond. The ship's carpenter fashioned a wooden ball and a couple of bats. There were certain difficulties that had to be overcome. A Portuguese seaman, appointed to the job of umpiring, had trouble learning the rules. He only learned, for example, the part about calling strikes, and couldn't seem to remember that there were also balls. At last they impeached him out of his job and put him in the outfield, and named the cook as umpire.

After their rescue and return to Boston, the men told reporters that they played baseball almost constantly from dawn to dark.

THE FANS used to laugh at Mike Kreevich when he was with the Chicago White Sox. Said he was a trifle daft. "He claims," they said, "that he's got left-handed bats and right-handed bats."

His teammates, however, didn't kid Mike about it. They

knew he had good reason to use different bats against left-handed pitchers and right-handed pitchers. Whenever he faced a southpaw, he found most of the pitches came down the inside; when he faced a right-hander, the ball usually was thrown on the outside. So his right-handed bat was a trifle longer than his left-handed bat. Crazy? Like a Foxx.

OUT OF THE HERDS of psychiatrists now infesting the land come occasional pronouncements on the subject of baseball. We should listen to them, and find out the underlying significance of the game. No sense in just going out to see somebody win a ball game. Here is the professional observation of a New York psychiatrist:

"A baseball game forms a mass catharsis of great curative value in ironing out our mental quirks and is of definite therapeutic value from a psychiatrist's viewpoint. It has good therapeutic value because it is available in a democratic way to the rich and poor alike.

"Baseball parks provide a kindergarten for adults. Our child-like and adolescent emotions, pent up in a panic-stricken world filled with taboos, find a harmless release through vicarious participation in the game."

RULE NO. 58 in the book says: "Under no circumstances shall a manager, captain, or player dispute the accuracy of the umpire's judgment and decision on a play." That's the official law of the game and that's why we never see a manager, captain, or player disputing the accuracy of the umpire's judgment and decision on a play.

Joe Engel, the unpredictable boss of the Chattanooga club, was not the team's manager and therefore didn't come under this regulation. Joe, being president of the club, usually sat in a box, and when he was unhappy about the judgment and decision of an umpire, he usually said so in tones audible in Memphis.

One day during a game on the home grounds Joe grew so disputatious that he was yelling protests in the direction of the plate umpire after every ball that was pitched. Finally the ump called a Chattanooga player out on strikes and braced himself for the explosion from Joe Engel's box. Hearing nothing, the umpire turned his head and glanced toward the box. There sat Joe—actually frothing at the mouth. The umpire learned later that Joe had taken some water in his mouth, then chucked in a handful of Bromo-Seltzer.

OLD NEWSPAPER FILES tell the story of a man who collapsed one afternoon in the grandstand at Philadelphia, victim of a heart attack brought on by the excitement of a game between the Athletics and Cleveland.

The game went into the ninth inning with the Athletics leading 3 to 0. Then the Cleveland team came to life in the top of the ninth. The Indians scored two runs, then filled the bases. With two men out, that was the situation prevailing when the spectator collapsed. He was taken in an unconscious condition to a hospital. He lay unconscious all through the night and then around dawn opened his eyes. He was able to murmur a question to the nurse. Did Cleveland win it? The nurse didn't know, but hurried out of the room and came back to tell him:

"The last man at bat was struck out and the Athletics won, 3 to 2."

The patient smiled, closed his eyes again, and died.

AN UMPIRE named Drubinka, working in the Alabama State League, was behind the plate in a game between Troy and Greenville when one of the batters began yelling and kicking dirt over a called strike. The batter kept up his bellowing longer than usual and finally Umpire Drubinka took hold of him and said:

"Now, just a minute, son. Take it easy. I want to show you something."

The umpire pulled a deck of playing cards out of his hip pocket. Fanning the cards out, he extended the deck toward the batter, told him to take one of the cards, look at it, and keep its face concealed. The player did so.

"You got the ten of diamonds," said Umpire Drubinka.

The batter, astonished at the call, had now forgotten his big beef about the called strike.

"How'd you ever figure that out?" he demanded.

"The same way I figured that last pitch was a strike," snapped the umpire. "Now let's play ball and leave smart matters to smart people."

OWNERS OF National League clubs in 1897 were distressed by the unusual number of violent rhubarbs that cropped up all during the season. Later on, however, they were inclined to be grateful for all those ructions on the playing fields.

The league had a rule under which all money collected from players in fines went into a fund which was used, after the season ended, to finance the annual banquet held by the club owners. By the end of the 1897 season, ballplayers had been so disorderly that a fund of $1,400 had accumulated toward the purchase of liquor and food, and the banquet was a staggering success.

THE ST. JOSEPH TEAM in the Western League once had a second baseman renowned as a slugger but somewhat inept as a fielder. His standard technique was to let the ball hit his chest, drop to the ground, and then pick it up for the throw. The trouble was he sometimes couldn't pick it up fast enough. On one particular afternoon he had such a rough time getting his hand on the ball that four errors were charged against him. The following day, an anonymous fan sent him a package containing a baseball to which had been fastened a leather loop cut from a dog's leash. "Here's a ball," wrote the sarcastic fan, "that you ought to be able to hang onto."

IN THE MIDDLE of the 1950 season an Old-timers' Day was held at the Polo Grounds featuring a three-inning exhibition between a team of creaking ex-Giants and another made up of the crumbling remains of the old St. Louis Gashouse Gang. This double reunion produced some memorable incidents, such as Pepper Martin's unexpected explanation of himself on a pre-game television program conducted by Laraine Day. Miss Day asked the aging Wild Horse of the Osage just what quality it was within him that made him one of the game's most spectacular and daring performers in the field and on the base paths. Old Pepper didn't hesitate over the answer. "I was able to do all those things," he said, "because I always kept the spirit of Christ right here in my heart."

During the game itself, the first Old Giant to get on base was suddenly trapped off the bag by the hidden-ball trick. The St. Louis first baseman seemed to return the ball to the pitcher, but when the Giant stepped off the base, he was tagged. An immediate ruction arose, the umpires rushed out, and it was found that the first baseman had a ball but so did the pitcher. At this point the umpires seized Leo Durocher, playing at short, and found a third ball in his hip pocket. Further search revealed a ball in the hip pocket of every Cardinal in the park.

The hidden-ball trick is a rare stratagem nowadays. However, if you run into Rabbit Maranville he'll tell you about the time it was worked on him twice in a single day. When he was with the Boston Braves Maranville got careless one afternoon and an infielder who had concealed the ball in his glove tagged him out. The victim was kidded unmercifully by his

teammates for several hours afterward, and then the matter was dropped. That evening Maranville and several other players were at a table in the dining room of their hotel. Someone suggested that a very wonderful sort of dessert could be had by asking for the chef's special. Maranville promptly ordered it. It certainly looked special when it came—a large mound of ice cream with whipped cream and cherries. When the Rabbit dug into it, of course, he found a hidden ball.

CASEY STENGEL sometimes gets to talking about tired outfielders. He is inclined to be sympathetic in his attitude toward outfielders who have to run themselves ragged because a pitcher is being belted all over the premises. Casey has been there.

When he was playing with the Phillies, Stengel remembers the day his club's manager chose to try out several of his rookie pitchers. Casey was playing the outfield and the opposition batters were making mincemeat of the Philadelphia rookies. In one particular inning the ball was being whaled by every man who came to the plate, and Casey found himself racing first to the right, then to the left, until he was so pooped he knew he couldn't keep it up much longer. He was standing out there, panting and sweating and thinking that maybe he ought to find some more congenial life's work for himself, when the crack of the bat sounded once again. The ball soared over his head and went to the wall, and Casey ran after it to the best of his feeble ability. Picking it up, he saw he wouldn't be able to prevent the runner from scoring an inside-the-park home run. So he didn't throw it at all. With the ball in his hand, he trudged slowly in from the field, across the diamond and up to the plate. There he handed the ball to the catcher.

"Listen," he said, "do me a favor. Take this ball and hold onto it awhile. Don't give it to anybody and don't throw it to anybody till I get back to right field. I got to get a breather one way or another or I'll not last the inning."

And so the catcher hung onto the ball as Casey strolled slowly back to his position.

Fifteen years later Stengel, then manager of the Brooklyn Dodgers, came into Philadelphia for a series with the Phillies in their little bandbox of a ball park, Baker Bowl, which has since been torn down. The right-field fence in the park was almost within spitting distance of the plate; it was faced with tin and when the batters were hot, the clatter and bang of balls hit against that fence could be heard for half a mile.

For the first game of the series Casey chose a pitcher named Walter Beck. The Philadelphia boys took kindly to Beck's offerings and line drives were soon banging against that tin wall. Hack Wilson was playing right field for the Dodgers and by the middle of the game he was wore to a frazzle. Then Casey decided Pitcher Beck might be better off under a shower. Time was called as Casey ambled out to the mound. In right field Hack Wilson took advantage of the recess, walked over to a shady spot, sat down on the grass and let his head droop to denote weariness.

At the mound Stengel informed Beck that he was through for the day and Beck put up a loud argument against being removed. He got so mad, in fact, that when Casey insisted he had to go, the young man whirled around and heaved the ball furiously into right field. Bang! It hit that tin fence. Off the ground came Hack Wilson, saying to himself, no doubt, "My God! Another one!"

Hack scampered after the ball, fielded it, and pegged it into second to keep a nonexistent runner from stretching a nothing into a double.

AN UMPIRE named Gordon, working in the Illinois-Indiana-Iowa League, may deserve mention in the definitive history of baseball as the only umpire ever to put a sports writer out of a game.

Gordon was working a game at Springfield and had just called a third strike on one of the home team's batsmen when a torrent of abuse came down upon him. Gordon thought that he had heard all the words, but now somebody up there in the stands was uttering profanities that were new even to an umpire's asbestos ears. Gordon whirled around and spotted the eloquent individual—a sports writer in the press box.

The umpire called time. Then he called a couple of policemen. Then he called officials of the Springfield club. To this group he announced his sentiments in strong terms. He said that if the obscene stinker in the press box was not thrown out of the park at once, he would forfeit the game to the visiting team and compel the Springfield management to refund all admission money.

The sports writer was thrown out.

THE YANKEES were playing the Senators one steaming afternoon in Griffith Stadium and the stands were packed. Came a lull when the teams were changing sides after the fifth inning. Then from the loud-speakers came the voice of the park announcer:

"Will the ladies and gentlemen in the boxes please remove their garments?"

It was hot enough, and some of the ladies and gentlemen would gladly have complied. Most of them realized, however, that the announcer had meant for them to remove their jackets from the railing.

IN HIS LONG CAREER as an active player Freddie Fitzsimmons either witnessed or took part in many a brawl growing out of the ancient rivalry between the Dodgers and the Giants. Freddie played for one side or the other for something like fifteen years. And if you ask him which game between the teams stands out foremost in his memory, he'll tell you about one in which not a single angry blow was struck.

The Dodgers were playing at the Polo Grounds in the middle 1930s and Freddie was pitching for the Giants. Things were moving along on an even keel until Babe Herman came to bat in one of the late innings. Freddie pitched to Babe and the next thing he remembered a lot of ballplayers were standing around him and someone was giving him something strong to smell. Herman had slammed the ball straight back at Freddie. It had hit him in the ribs. Freddie couldn't remember having done it, but he reached for the ball as by instinct, threw Herman out at first, and then sagged to the ground. His throw retired the side and he was led off the field to the dugout where, in a few minutes, he was feeling better. Still a trifle woozy, he went up to take his turn at bat. The Brooklyn pitcher threw the ball and, once again, everything went black. The ball had hit Freddie on the side of the head and for the second time in ten minutes he was knocked unconscious. This time he decided he had had enough and, as soon as he was able to navigate, went on home.

BILL DINEEN was pitching and Lou Criger was catching for the St. Louis Browns one day in 1909 with their club two runs ahead in the eighth inning. The visiting team filled the bases with two out, and Pitcher Dineen went to work earnestly on the next batter. Trying to put some special stuff on the ball, he unleashed a wild one. The ball was beyond the reach of Criger's glove, shot back against the base of the grandstand wall, and bounced toward the visitors' dugout.

Pitcher Dineen, of course, charged down off the mound to cover home. Catcher Criger was in hot pursuit of the vagrant ball. It came to a stop directly in front of the visitors' bench. Somebody in the dugout, with a great idea, moved fast. He stepped out quickly with a canvas bag full of baseballs. He turned the bag upside down and poured baseballs on top of the ball that was in play.

Catcher Criger arrived. One run had already scored. He hesitated only a moment, staring at the assortment of balls on the ground, then snatched one of them up and fired it to the pitcher at the plate, and the second runner was tagged before he could hit the dish.

"Safe!" yelled the umpire. He was, to be sure, immediately surrounded by loudly indignant St. Louis Browns.

"He didn't throw the ball that was in play," insisted the umpire.

"How do you know I didn't?" demanded Catcher Criger.

"It's up to you," argued the umpire, "to prove that you did throw the right one. You couldn't prove it. Nobody could prove it."

The rhubarb raged on, with the St. Louis team charging

flagrant interference, but by this time they had called the umpire such an assortment of unpleasant names that he was displeased with them, and stood his ground—the runner had been tagged with the wrong ball, and the run was legal. And that's the way it went into the books.

DOWN IN THE EVANGELINE LEAGUE a few years ago two umpires, assigned to handle a game between Alexandria and Hammond, failed to show up. Rather than call the game off, it was agreed that a local sand-lot umpire do the calling.

The amateur ump got along fine until the eighth inning when an Alexandria batter sent a line drive over the third sack. The ball landed close to the foul line and went on into the corner. Both managers, Carl Kott of Alexandria and Babe Benning of Hammond, closed in on the fill-in umpire, demanding to know whether he had called the ball fair or foul.

"Gentlemen," replied the umpire, "I honestly don't know what it was. It was just too hard to tell from here."

The managers looked at one another. It had been their idea to use this fellow as an umpire; it was up to them to be reasonable. They decided that the question should be settled by flipping a coin. A quarter was tossed in the air, came down heads, and the batter was given a two-base hit and Alexandria was credited with the two runs that had crossed the plate.

SATCHEL PAIGE, the great Negro pitcher, used to be available for duty in the outfield. If his team ran short of outfielders, Old Satch had no objection to taking his glove and going to the picket line, where he did a capable job of fielding.

One day, during a tour in Venezuela, this need arose and Satch went to right field. Beyond the normal fielding area lay a swampy area covered with a thick tangle of undergrowth. During the game one of the Venezuelan players hit a long drive that got past Satch and rolled into the edge of this swamp. Satch galloped up to the point where the ball entered the brush. Suddenly he stopped, whirled like a ballet dancer, and took off at top speed for the dugout.

His eyes were popping and his breath was short when he arrived and he announced that the biggest snake in the world had almost got him. One of his teammates, who had ranged out in that direction when he saw Satch hadn't got the ball, verified the story. This one said the snake was "big as a telephone pole." Said Satch: "Bigger."

After that Satch never played the outfield again. He argued that it was unlucky for him to do anything but stay within sixty feet of home plate and pitch.

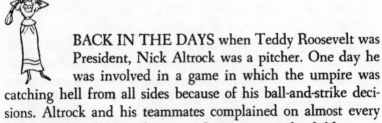

BACK IN THE DAYS when Teddy Roosevelt was President, Nick Altrock was a pitcher. One day he was involved in a game in which the umpire was catching hell from all sides because of his ball-and-strike decisions. Altrock and his teammates complained on almost every ball pitched, whether they were batting or in the field.

About halfway through the game Altrock was on the bench when there was a commotion in one of the field boxes. A spectator had fainted. Nick grabbed up the tin water bucket and dipper, standard dugout equipment, and rushed over to the stricken man. He sloshed water in his face and then gave him a drink.

On his way back to the bench Nick passed near the umpire, who asked him what had happened.

"The guy didn't say much," Nick replied, "but his wife said ·you called two pitches in a row the way they oughta been called so he just keeled over from shock."

RED ORMSBY always said it was a base canard and a damn lie. Red served as a big-league umpire for many years. In 1935 he began hearing of a terrible story that was being circulated among ballplayers with himself as the principal character.

According to the story Red's decisions had angered the fans in a certain city and they had been threatening physical violence when the cops took over. One policeman, according to the story, escorted the umpire from the field.

The way the story was being told, the policeman remarked at the time: "I'm just doing my official duty in aiding the blind."

Red said it never happened at all and, further than that, he had good eyesight.

GEORGE SISLER was on third and Goose Goslin was on second for Washington in a game quite a few years ago. The Goose, famous for his competitive spirit, was figuring that, given a slight break, he was going to score. The pitcher was a rookie, so Goslin took himself a long lead off second base. Half step by half step he continued edging down the line until he was almost midway to third. Meanwhile Sisler was taking a shorter lead off third.

The pitcher went into his motion and Goslin decided to go. He went on down to third at top speed and slid into the bag. He was surprised that nobody made an effort to tag him; he was also surprised to find George Sisler standing on third. Then the ball arrived and the third baseman tagged both men, to make certain one of them was out.

There was a lot of whooping and yelling from the stands, but above the commotion came a fog-horn shout. It was Joe Cantillon, former manager of the Washington club, who was present as a spectator.

"No matter what anybody says," yelled Joe, "I don't blame you for trying to steal! *Look at the lead you had!*"

TIM HURST, one of the most colorful characters who ever wore an umpire's uniform, once thumbed a player out of a game without knowing what offense the player had committed.

Germany Schaefer, second baseman for Detroit and himself a screwball of fair magnitude, was at bat and Tim was back of the plate.

Suddenly most of the Cleveland players in the field began laughing. Tim Hurst, who believed that ball games should be played in an aura of dignity, whipped off his mask and glanced around, seeking the reason for the hilarity.

In a moment he was able to decide that the Cleveland players were laughing at Germany Schaefer, but Tim couldn't see Schaefer's face, so he was still mystified.

"Schaefer," he demanded, "what are ye up to now?"

Schaefer turned with a look of innocence and hurt on his face, but by this time the umpire had made up his mind.

"You're outa the game!" he bellowed.

"What on earth for?" demanded Schaefer.

"I don't know what for," replied Hurst, "but you're out."

The umpire didn't learn until after the game that he had been correct in his judgment. Schaefer had gone up to bat with a stage-prop mustache in his hand and, while facing away from Hurst, had stuck it on his upper lip and gone into a series of fantastic grimaces. He had managed to remove it before turning around to give Tim that innocent look.

AN EIGHTEEN-YEAR-OLD BOY was brought before City Judge R. A. Myatt in Knoxville one day in 1938, charged with larceny. The city attorney explained that the young man was standing in the street back of the grandstand at the ball park when a foul ball came over the roof and dropped to the pavement. The boy picked it up and started away with it, but he was caught and placed under arrest for taking property that didn't belong to him.

Judge Myatt now spoke.

"As we all know," he said, "the Knoxville team is in last place in the Southern Association. I am not so sure but what it would be a good thing if all their baseballs were taken away from them for a while. A layoff might bring them out of their slump. At any rate, they would do much better if they quit fouling so many pitches over the grandstand. Case dismissed."

ELMIRA and Williamsport were engaged in an Eastern League game some years ago and Elmira got the bases loaded with only one out. The next batter hit a ground ball to third. The third baseman grabbed the ball and stepped on the bag, forcing the runner who had been on second. Then he threw to first. The ball went over the first baseman's head and all the Elmira runners kept going—including the man who had been forced at third.

The first baseman retrieved the ball and threw to the plate just as this particular runner—the one who had been forced out—was coming in. The catcher tagged him and the umpire declared him out.

Nobody seemed to notice that one base runner had been called out twice, and the Elmira players took the field. Then someone called the umpire's attention to the fact that he had called a man out who was already out. This meant, it was contended, that only two legal outs had been made and Elmira should still be at bat.

The umpire decided otherwise. He said that man shouldn't have been running around the bases, making like he was a live runner; he had interfered with the normal progress of the game, therefore both of his outs counted.

It was an unusual ruling and, strangely enough, met with only mild opposition from the Elmira team. They seemed satisfied to forget about it and proceed with the contest.

IT MAY HAVE LOOKED peculiar to people in the stands, but whenever Rube Waddell got close to a spare baseball that might have been lying around on the ground, someone always seemed to sneak out quickly and grab it before the Rube could get his hands on it.

The great pitcher had a sort of hobby of collecting spare baseballs. He was a man inclined to spend considerable time with his foot on a brass rail, and he was usually broke. He was a hero in many barrooms but he also had a reputation in those resorts as a man who frequently tried to get drinks without paying for them.

It was his custom, then, on leaving the ball park to make his way to some pub where, of course, he'd be immediately recognized. He'd stand around a bit, chinning with the proprietor and the customers and then he'd manage to steer the conversation around to one of his spectacular pitching victories.

"Funny thing," he'd then say, "I just happen to have the very ball I used in that game right here in my pocket. How'd you like to have it, propilly autographed?"

"Gee, Rube, that'd be somethin'!" they'd usually say.

As soon as he had autographed the ball and handed it over, the bartender naturally poured a few free ones.

And that was why they had to keep an eye on Rube in the ball park, lest he steal every baseball in sight.

AN UMPIRE named Murray, working in the American Association, acquired a sort of distinction one afternoon during a game at Louisville. Murray had been calling balls and strikes to the best of his ability but not to the satisfaction of the Louisville fans. They began expressing their displeasure by throwing fruits, vegetables, shoes, bottles, and other articles in his direction. Murray bore up courageously under this bombardment—and then a hatchet whizzed past his head. That was too much. He called time and demanded that the police go find the heartless human who had let fly with the hatchet.

They located the man—a carpenter who had stopped at the park on his way home from work, carrying his kit of tools with him.

THE CITY OF TEXARKANA is confusing enough without the help of eccentric ballplayers. Part of the town is in Texas and part in Arkansas, and a fellow might suddenly find himself violating the Mann Act in five minutes. Well, maybe six minutes.

Four or five years ago Texarkana was playing a team from Sherman. The game was a scoreless tie going into the last of the ninth. There were two out, a man on third, and two strikes on the Texarkana batter.

The runner on third decided it was a good moment for him to try to steal home. On the next pitch he came racing down the line. The Sherman catcher made a great try but the umpire called the runner safe. This should have been the signal for everybody to go on home, but nothing of the sort happened.

The Sherman manager came charging out, demanding to know whether that last pitch had been a ball or a strike. If it was a strike, the run didn't count, because the batter would have been out and the side retired. Both the plate umpire and the base umpire admitted that they hadn't watched the pitch itself—they had been occupied watching the runner coming down from third. Now the president of the East Texas League came out of his box seat and announced that the run did not count. Whereupon the plate umpire slammed his mask on the ground and resigned from his job. The league president stood his ground, and announced that the game would be resumed on the following day, beginning with the tenth inning.

Sherman scored two runs in the first of the tenth on the morrow, but Texarkana got four in their half and, in the words of their manager, won the game twice.

DETROIT was playing the Yankees one June day in 1948 at Briggs Stadium. In the sixth inning with Allie Reynolds on the mound, Dick Wakefield came to bat for Detroit. He faced the pitcher, then took his bat off his shoulder and started walking out toward the mound. The spectators thought he had gone crazy, for as he walked toward Reynolds, he began swinging his bat wildly through the air. People figured Wakefield had suddenly blown his top and was going out to bludgeon the Yankee pitcher.

Then word got around that Wakefield wasn't after Reynolds. He was after gnats. A thick swarm of the tiny insects had come into the park and had settled down at a spot midway

between the mound and the plate. Being ignorant of baseball, the gnats didn't realize that they were in hazardous territory. So they clung to that spot. The spectators couldn't see them, but both Wakefield and Pitcher Reynolds could. And it was Wakefield who decided to get them out of the way, having no desire to try to hit a ball coming out of a fog. His maneuver was effective, driving the bugs away, and then on the next pitch he belted a double.

THE LOUISVILLE CLUB was in spring training camp, quite a few years ago, when a young man arrived for a tryout with the team. He was given a uniform and sent to the outfield, where he put on a passable demonstration of running and catching flies.

When he came in from the field one of the Louisville coaches asked him, "What playing position do you like the most?"

"Well," said the young man, "it's hard to say. Most of the time I just kinda lean forward a little and put my hands on my knees, but sometimes I get tired of that and just stand up straight for a while."

THE CINCINNATI REDS were having a miserable season back in the 1880s and the fans were staying away from the ball park. Public interest in the team, in fact, was so low that paid admissions were scarcely sufficient to pay for the bills on the ballplayers' caps.

There remained at least one loyal individual. He was a sports writer for a Cincinnati newspaper and though he found it difficult to write cheerfully about the team, he continued to search for optimistic news, and even to invent some of it. He began writing about certain "new faces" that would soon appear in the line-up, suggesting that the club management was getting ready to bring in some fresh and brilliant talent.

Before long the sports writer was faced with the necessity of being more specific about the new faces; so now he began writing about a phenomenal shortstop who was dickering with the Reds' management. He never named this shortstop, of course, but continued writing about him in a mysterious way for five or six days. At last, almost in desperation, he wrote that the new shortstop would take the field on the following afternoon.

A larger crowd than usual turned up at the ball park, attracted by the talk of this new shortstop who was a ball of fire. When the Cincinnati team took the field, all eyes were on the man who walked to the shortstop position. He was a sight. He had perhaps the biggest set of whiskers ever seen on a baseball diamond. In the warm-up period he whipped the ball around zestfully and appeared to be as skillful a fielder as the stories said.

Then, as the umpire called for the start of play, he suddenly yanked his whiskers off and stood revealed as Charlie Fulmer, the team's regular shortstop. Having exhibited his true identity to the crowd, he returned the beard to his chin and the game started. The fans were amused by the horseplay, but soon they were cheering. Shortstop Fulmer had turned into a ball of fire, playing a terrific game in the field and at bat. Further than that, most of the other Cincinnati players seemed to have taken on a new spirit. They embarked on an impressive winning streak and played excellent ball throughout the remainder of that season.

THE FOLLOWING news item appeared in a Brooklyn newspaper in 1903:

PICTURE OF BOTTLE
OF WHISKEY
IS CAUSE OF DEFEAT

Out in right field of the Brooklyn ball park a whiskey concern has painted a giant picture of a whiskey bottle to advertise its wares and this, according to certain of the Brooklyn players, has been the cause of recent defeats sustained by the club.

The colors, which are bright and many, run together in the vision of right-hand hitters and make it impossible to judge a curve ball.

Manager Hanlon has decided to have the bottle taken down.

THE FIRST INNING that Bucky Walters ever pitched in the major leagues belongs in the history of baseball because of an argument between a batter and a plate umpire. Bucky had been an infielder for the Phillies, but in 1934 he was converted into a pitcher and the day came for his debut on the mound in an exhibition game.

He walked the first batter. He hit the next one with the ball. He walked the next one. He walked the next one. He threw a wild pitch. He hit the next man with a pitched ball. Now the sixth man came up to face him. Somehow Bucky managed to get two strikes on the next batter. The next two pitches came straight at the batter's head, but he managed to duck out of the way, and the count was two and two. Bucky went into his windup. Down came the pitch.

"Ball three," said the umpire.

The batter whirled around.

"Ball three, hell!" he shouted. "That was a strike if I ever saw one! Came right acrost the plate! I'm out!"

"Okay," said the umpire, "if that's the way you want it, you're out, and you're also feeble-minded."

"That's what *you* think," said the batter. "My mama didn't raise any idiot childern. Not for a hatful of money will I stand up there and let that guy throw one more pitch at me. I'm out, and I'm *dern well happy to be out!*"

And slowly walked away.

FELLOW by the name of Polli, a coach for the Jacksonville club in the South Atlantic League, made a big hit with the fans one afternoon a few years back. When the time came for him to take his position in the coacher's box, Polli walked out carrying a straight-backed chair. He placed the chair within the white lines, sat down, and waited for activity to begin.

The plate umpire, the moment he saw Polli and the chair, scurried down to third and ordered the furniture off the field. Polli gave him a loud argument. He quoted the book at the umpire, demanding to be shown any rule that said he couldn't sit down if he felt like it.

"Listen," said the umpire, "I don't care what the book says. Next thing, you'll be wantin' to bring a sofy, or a feather bed, or a grand py-anna out here. Now, take that chair the hell back where you got it and, furthermore, you're fined ten dollars."

Polli had to yield, but the fine didn't bother him. The fans, grateful for the diversion he had furnished, took up a collection and paid it for him.

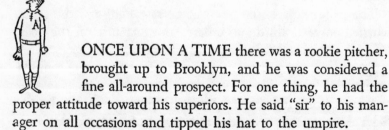 IN THE SUMMER of 1941 an umpire named Joliff, working in the Coastal Plain League, was seen in public wearing a small bandage on his head. Tongues began to wag. The story got around that Joliff had been waylaid by a gang of disgruntled players in Rocky Mount, and that the umpire had been hit on the head with a ball bat. As is usually the case, the story acquired much embroidery as it spread, and in due time it reached the ears of Ray H. Goodmon, president of the league. Mr. Goodmon summoned Umpire Joliff. Sure enough, his head was bandaged.

"Tell me the truth, now," said the president. "Who did it?"

"I did it," said Joliff. He said that he had made the mistake of straightening up suddenly while walking beneath the grandstand, and had cracked his head on a steel girder.

Which proves that the sight of an umpire in bandages doesn't *necessarily* mean that destiny, in the form of ballplayers, has caught up with him.

ONCE UPON A TIME there was a rookie pitcher, brought up to Brooklyn, and he was considered a fine all-around prospect. For one thing, he had the proper attitude toward his superiors. He said "sir" to his manager on all occasions and tipped his hat to the umpire.

In one of his first games as a big-leaguer, this polite young man was pitching against the St. Louis Cardinals. The contest got into the last half of the ninth with the Cardinals at bat. The score was tied at six all, and the Cardinals had a runner on third.

Miller Huggins, then manager of the St. Louis club, was coaching at third base. The young pitcher was taking his time on the mound, and had about made up his mind to go to work on the batter. Then he heard a voice, a voice that had authority in it. He glanced over toward third, just as Huggins called out to him: "Hey, son, let's have a look at that ball!"

The young man, as indicated, had respect for his elders. There stood Miller Huggins, his hands outstretched to catch the ball, so the pitcher tossed it over to him. Huggins, however, didn't catch it. He dropped his hands and stepped quickly to one side, letting the ball roll to the stand. And the Cardinal runner scampered in to score the winning run for St. Louis.

BILLY SOUTHWORTH needed a run badly. His St. Louis Cardinals were tied up with Cincinnati and the game was in the late stages. The Cardinals had two men on base, with one out, but the batter now at the plate was a poor hitter. When he had two strikes on him, Southworth decided he'd try a pinch hitter next. He glanced around the dugout and his mind settled on Pepper Martin, out of the game because of a minor injury.

"Feel okay to go up there?" asked Southworth.

Pepper gave him an eager nod and Southworth returned his attention to home plate. As he had anticipated, the batter was an easy out. Southworth was studying the situation on the field. A minute or two passed and then it occurred to him that his pinch hitter hadn't gone to the plate. He glanced around again and saw his pinch hitter, Mr. Pepper Martin, stretched at full length on the floor of the dugout, unconscious as a fence post.

Pepper, as always, had reacted to the order with typical zest and eagerness. The moment Southworth told him to get ready, he had leaped from the bench toward the bat rack, struck his head on the concrete roof of the dugout, and was knocked cold. He regained consciousness shortly after the Cardinals had won the game.

IF THERE WAS EVER any occasion for histrionics, Charlie Grimm was not the man to pass it up. Back in 1946 Charlie's Chicago Cubs were engaged in a tight contest. They started a rally in the eighth inning and loaded the bases. Phil Cavarretta was on third, Andy Pafko on second, and Marv Rickert on first.

The next batter let the first pitch go by, and Rickert made a try at stealing second. Out in the third-base coacher's box Charlie Grimm saw two of his men snarled up on second base, with the ball coming down to get one of them for certain; and before Charlie could make up his mind about anything, Cavarretta left third and tried to reach the plate, but the ball got back there in time and he was tagged out, and there was much general confusion. When the excitement had died down a bit, most people cut their eyes over toward third to see how Charlie was taking all this tragedy. He was stretched at full length on the ground, his hands covering his eyes, his feet kicking the dirt. And the noises he was making, according to people sitting within a half mile of him, were straight off the sound track of a jungle movie.

HOW DOES a great big fancy King react to baseball? Thirty-some years ago the Giants and the White Sox visited London during a world tour and played an exhibition game with George V as a spectator.

John McGraw sat beside the monarch and made an effort to explain the play as it went along. King George seemed to understand everything, saying "Ummmm" as each maneuver was explained.

Finally a situation arose in which a White Sox player was called upon to bunt. The sacrifice was successful.

"That, Your Majesty," said McGraw, "is called a sacrifice. It is called a sacrifice because the batter sacrificed himself for the other man, permitting the other man to advance from first base to second base."

The King nodded and stared at the man who had sacrificed, watching him as he returned from first base. At last the King spoke one of the few sentences he uttered all through the game. He said:

"Rawther sporting of the gentleman, what?"

"I TELL YA," said the old man sitting on the nail keg in the hardware store, "these here are bad times. Immoral times. Wimmin goin' around 'thout enough clothes on to wad a musket. Fellers writin' books with cuss-words in 'em. Young kids outa the eighth grade duckin' up side roads and lollygaggin' all over the place. What kind of a guvment we got lets things like that go on? Got so baseball is gittin' immoral. Ten er twelve year ago ballplayers wanted to congratulate one another, er in-courage one another, they'd slap one another on the shoulder. Ever notice what they do now—invariable? Slap one another on the bee-hime! Right in front of everbody! Do it all the time. I tell ya, when I was a young fella, a ballplayer slapped another ballplayer on the bee-hime, he'd a been put outa the game fer indecency."

AFTER MANY ILLUSTRIOUS YEARS as an important figure in the game, Gabby Hartnett came close to quitting baseball forever one afternoon in May at Jersey City. Gabby was manager of the Jersey City club, which was playing Syracuse, and midway of the contest Gabby's blood vessels swole up over a decision made and rendered by Umpire Swanson. Gabby stormed onto the field, squawking his discontent, and Umpire Swanson told him to shut up, whereupon Gabby snatched off his own cap and threw it high in the air.

"That'll cost you ten bucks," said the umpire. Gabby now opened all stops and shrieked about his constitutional rights, and uttered words that were purple and red, and the umpire thumbed him out of the game.

Meanwhile Jewel Ens, manager of the Syracuse team, had come quietly out of the dugout, a sly grin on his face. He picked up Gabby's cap. Then he scooped up a heaping handful of dirt and quietly dropped it into the cap and after that he put the cap back down on the turf.

When he had finished his tirade, Gabby stomped over and snatched the cap off the ground and slapped it on his head, and the dirt cascaded down over his face and neck and shoulders. He came, now, as near to internal combustion as it's possible without actual explosion. It wasn't so much the roaring laughter of the crowd—it was that dastard Umpire Swanson, standing there chuckling. As he made his way into exile, slapping dirt off his neck, Gabby was shouting that he'd never set foot on another baseball field as long as he lived—a resolution he later reconsidered.

A BIG CROWD turned out at the Dallas ball park one April night in 1949. Dallas and Oklahoma City were to play that evening, but there was to be an added attraction. President R. W. Burnett of the Dallas club had let word get around that he had a little surprise for the local fans, but nobody in the stands seemed to have any idea what it would be.

Just before time for the ball game to start, the park organist began playing "Three Blind Mice." Then out of the clubhouse, marching single file, came a line of umpires—thirty-four of them altogether. They paraded silently onto the field, lined up facing the grandstand, the organ music stopped and then in unison they let go with a tremendous "Boo!" It was probably the first time in history that umpires have had the pleasure of booing the fans.

The thirty-four umps were associated with the West Texas-New Mexico, East Texas, Big State, Rio Grande Valley and Longhorn leagues, and they had been attending a meeting in Dallas for the purpose of working out their season assignments.

 YOU NEVER KNOW what you can get away with in this world unless you make a try. The Yankees were playing the Red Sox at Fenway Park in the opening game of the 1949 season. The Yankees were at bat in the eighth inning and out in the right-field grandstand a teen-age boy made a decision. He was an autograph monster, and there on the grass, not too far away, were some people whose signatures he yearned to have in his little book. So over the barrier he came. He ran up to Outfielder Tom O'Brien first. Tom, a rookie, spoke sharply to him—this was not the time nor the place for such shenanigans. The kid to him said nuts, and raced over to Ted Williams. Ted took off his glove and signed. Next to Dom DiMaggio. Dom took off his glove and signed. Thirty-five thousand fans sat back and waited. Finally the boy scampered back to his place and the game was resumed. So far as is known, nobody uttered a word of remonstrance to him.

LEO DUROCHER'S famous observation that "nice guys finish last" doesn't set him apart from all other ballplayers. There have been many like Leo who, polite and even soft-spoken off the diamond, have had no use for the social prescriptions of Emily Post once they got into uniform.

John Smith was an outfielder for the St. Louis Cardinals in 1916—as nice a guy as you'd want to meet until he was engaged in the act of playing baseball. One day the Cards were playing the Cubs at Chicago and John was on second. Albert Betzel came to bat, took a terrific swipe at a slow pitch, and the bat flew out of his hands. It skittered across the infield past third base. Playing third for Chicago was Heinie Zimmerman. Heinie figured it would be chivalrous for him to go over and get the bat and return it to Betzel. As soon as he turned and started toward it, John Smith came charging down from second to third. At this point Heinie abandoned genteel behavior and set up a mighty howl to the umpire.

"My God!" he yelled. "I was just bein' nice and goin' out to pick up that bat. This guy's got no right to take a base on me!"

"You didn't call time," said the ump. "Nothing I can do about it."

Heinie now appealed to Smith himself, as a man of honor, and Smith just grinned and retained his position on third. A bit later he scored the run that won the game for the Cardinals.

Thirty-one years later the Cubs were in another game, this time with the Dodgers, and a similar situation arose. Pee Wee Reese was on first and Dixie Walker was at bat. Walker swung hard and the bat flew out toward the spot where Reese was taking his lead. Pee Wee stepped over to pick it up and throw it back toward the plate. As he was bending over, Clyde McCullough, the Cubs' catcher, fired the ball down to Eddie Waitkus at first, and Eddie walked over and tagged Pee Wee out. The Cubs, you see, had learned their lesson.

THE BRITISH, by long tradition, have always been confused by the American game of baseball. One aspect of this confusion was discussed in a letter to the New York *Times* in 1940. The letter was postmarked Washington, D.C., was signed "Pyecroft Ben-Pye" and read in part as follows:

"One becomes conscious that what is called 'the baseball season' has begun in this your native land. Whereupon one becomes semiconscious as one seeks to interpret the lingo, argot, cant, slang, and nonce terms in which sports writers self-consciously seek to bury from most of us whatever information might have been disclosed. Why such scribal crypticism?

"This morning, Lieutenant Sir Baldwin Inchcape Inchbald, C.D., displayed to me the reports in the newspapers about the professional games of yesterday. Sir Baldwin is my staff expert on Americanisms, but was in some degree nonplussed by the solecisms with which even otherwise estimable journals are rife today in setting forth the games of yesterday."

Listen here, Pyecroft! Go square leg yourself and mid off a couple of bails! With your googly!

AFTER A CAREER of umpiring, George Moriarty woke up one day to find himself a big-league manager—skipper of the Detroit Tigers. On the first road trip after Moriarty took over, the Tigers arrived in Washington for a series.

In the first game the Tigers found themselves trailing the Senators in the seventh. Manager Moriarty, sweating under the prospect of having his team shut out, went down to the third-base coaching box, hoping to have some traffic to handle at that point.

The first Detroit batter got a single, and Moriarty now hung up the hit-and-run sign. It worked nicely. The batter smacked a single to right. The runner already on base had taken a big lead off first and now went winging around second. Moriarty waved frantically for him to keep running.

Meanwhile the Washington right fielder had come in fast to grab the ball and cut loose a perfect peg to third. The ball and the runner arrived at third base in a photo finish.

Crouched over the play was the umpire. And as the ball came in, Moriarty himself went into a similar crouch. The third baseman grabbed the throw and swept his arm down to tag the runner as he came sliding in.

The umpire spread his arms and yelled, "Safe!"

And Moriarty, forgetting in the excitement who he was,

jerked his thumb and yelled, at the same moment, "Yer out!"

He hung his head in embarassment for a while after that, but he had presence of mind enough to agree that the legal umpire had been altogether correct in his decision.

THE NEW YORK YANKEES are capable of indulging in frivolity. You could win a bet by wagering that a ball has been hit over the center-field wall at the Yankee Stadium. The feat was accomplished on July 29, 1949, by Yogi Berra. Yogi did the trick during a pregame special presentation "directed by Thomas D. Henrich and George H. Stirnweiss." Messrs. Henrich and Stirnweiss announced that the Yankee catcher would knock a ball over that fence, and knock it he did. He simply walked out to center field, took a fungo bat, and let one go.

Among the other bits on the pre-game presentation:

Bill Dickey's cocker spaniel put on an exhibition of catching and chasing balls; the dog's speed of foot and unerring mouth work impressed everyone. He would become, it was proclaimed, the greatest shortstop in the game as soon as Mr. Dickey taught him to throw to first.

Ed Lopat walked onto the field wearing a heavy overcoat and was introduced as "the hottest pitcher in baseball today."

THE CROWD will always take to a man who can run faster than other men. A case in point is that of John B. (Hans) Lobert, who had a pair of the most remarkable legs in the history of baseball. Hans played with the Pirates, the Cubs, the Reds, the Phillies, and the Giants; his career as a player spanned the years 1903 to 1917. And his speed of foot was always getting him into crazy sorts of contests.

At the close of the 1913 season he went on a world tour with the White Sox and the Giants, and no matter where the Americans landed, Lobert's reputation had preceded him and people wanted to see him scamper.

Before starting across the Pacific the two teams arrived at Oxnard, California, for an exhibition game. Arriving at Oxnard, Hans was told that arrangements had been made for him to run a race with a cow pony. Hans said okay.

That afternoon seven thousand spectators, many of them cowhands, assembled at the park. The race between Hans and the horse was to be run after the ball game, but the crowd began howling for it so that the game itself was halted in the seventh inning.

The horse, ridden by a cowboy, came on the field and Hans took his place at home plate. It was agreed that Hans would circle the bases in normal ballplayer fashion, and that the horse would run around the bases. Umpire Bill Klem was appointed official starter and judge. Horse and man stood at the plate, Klem fired the gun, and off they went.

Hans was a fast starter, got the jump on the cow pony, and was leading when he passed first base. He was still out in front going down to second. Heading for third, Hans went wide and the horse closed in on him. There were some who said the cowboy was nettled and trying to ride Hans down. They came to third base without mishap, however, and then down the homestretch toward the plate, running in what appeared to be a dead heat. As they crossed the finish line Bill Klem yelled that the horse had won. Now, Hans Lobert being a ballplayer, and Bill Klem being an umpire, a ruction was inevitable.

Hans took off his cap and threw it on the ground and howled: "Says who!"

"You lost by a nose!" roared Klem, and many people laughed, for Hans had perhaps the largest nose in organized baseball.

Hans kicked dirt, and swung his arms, and called names. The horse just stood by and smirked. And though Hans was unable to get Klem to reverse his decision, there were plenty of people in the crowd who swore that Hans had really won the race.

In 1917 at Havana, Hans ran an even more fantastic race. This time he was matched against two automobiles, two motorcycles, two horses and another man. It was, of course, a handicap affair, with a purse of $400 going to the winner. The race took place at the Oriental Park hoss track. The distance for the motorcycles was one mile; for the automobiles, seven eighths of a mile; for the horses, three quarters of a mile; for Hans Lobert, 535 yards, and for the other man, 450 yards. There was considerable betting on the race, with Lobert the ruling favorite. He opened at 2½ to 1 and at post time was quoted at 7 to 5.

The motorcycles were given the rail position. Next to them were the two horses, then the automobiles, and, on the outside, the humans. Hans broke fast, took the lead over all competition and stayed in the lead right down to the wire. One of the motorcycles was giving him fits and, as he approached his finish line, Hans realized that the machine might beat him. He knew he'd have to give his all, and he did. His all was a magnificent slide. When the dust settled, there lay the great Lobert, apparently unconscious. His wife rushed to his side, and right behind her came a gentleman who had won a roll on Hans's victory. The gentleman had a flask with him. He poured a slug of brandy into Hans and the victor got up and walked off the track.

For winning the race, Hans collected considerably more than the four-hundred-dollar purse. Christy Mathewson, John Mc-Graw, and Germany Schaefer were present and had wagered heavily on Hans. They split their winnings with him. And Mrs. Hans Lobert revealed, when it was all over, that she had laid a sizable chunk on Papa to whip the motorcycles, the automobiles, the horses, the other man, and any Cuban pigeons who happened along.

 ANDALUSIA AND BREWTON, two teams in the Alabama State League, were dueling on the diamond one July afternoon in 1947 when a run-down play between third and home developed. The trapped runner was Leslie McGarity, a quick-witted catcher for Brewton. The men who had him boxed in were John B. Hitson, the third baseman, and Jim Griffey, catcher for Andalusia.

Hitson got the ball first while McGarity was taking a long lead off third. Hitson threw to Catcher Griffey, and the two began closing in on their victim. Just as they were about to tag him, McGarity suddenly stopped and yelled, "Time!" The umpire, who was right on top of the play, threw up his hands and bellowed, "Time!" The two Andalusia players stared around in bewilderment while McGarity walked untouched back to third base, bent over and began fiddling with his shoestring.

Now the umpire had time to reconsider what had happened. Having reconsidered, his face grew red and, pointing at McGarity, he yelled, "You're out!"

"What for?" demanded McGarity. "Nobody tagged me."

"You're out," insisted the umpire, sputtering in anger, "for—for—for interference!"

"Interference with what?" demanded McGarity.

"Interference," screamed the livid umpire, "with—with— PROGRESS!"

And he made the decision stick.

IF YOU ARE ever walking outside a ball park and get hit by a home-run ball, and if you are one of those litigious persons who hollers for a lawyer before a doctor, here is a legal precedent you may call to your attorney's attention.

A dozen years ago a ball was hit out of the Louisville park, struck a boy and broke his nose. Litigation followed, and Judge Will H. Fulton of the Kentucky Court of Appeals eventually ruled:

"It is common knowledge that professional baseball players are trained and coached to knock the ball over the fence for a home run and that such a feat is not at all uncommon.

"Hence we are constrained to hold that the appellant [the Louisville Baseball Club] had notice that balls were often knocked over this fence into the public street and that such balls might strike or injure persons thereon."

All of which was the juridical manner of saying that home runs are hit on purpose. The kid got $2,000 for his broken nose.

 MANY BASEBALL FANS hold that the catcher is easily the most important man on any team, and the most admirable. In addition to taking all the assorted knocks that come with his job, he is the one man who must be on the alert constantly; he must control that ball and never lose it. Cat quickness is the attribute of a good catcher, and Frank Kerr of Milwaukee was a good catcher.

Kansas City was playing at Milwaukee one afternoon in 1948 and Frank Kerr was catching for the home team. Behind Frank stood Umpire Harry King, and on first base was a Kansas City runner, Leon Culberson. Catcher Kerr figured the runner was going to try a steal, so he signaled for a pitchout. The ball came in fast, struck the edge of his mitt, and shot over Kerr's shoulder.

Umpire King heard a loud clunk and felt a heavy blow that jerked his head back, but before he could collect his senses Catcher Kerr was climbing all over him. The ball had struck the umpire's mask and was wedged between the wires. Nothing's sacred, not even an umpire, to a catcher going after a ball. Kerr seized the mask and ripped it off Umpire King's head, almost taking his nose with it, and then he wrestled with the thing considerably, trying to get that ball out. Culberson made it to second with enough time left over to roast a goose. Milwaukee put up a holler, contending the ball was not in play while it was in the mask. But Umpire King ruled that in as much as the Milwaukee catcher had fielded *him* personally and then his mask and then the ball, it was *too* in play. And the run scored a bit later by Culberson proved to be the winning run for Kansas City.

A NEW YORK SPORTS WRITER sat in the Polo Grounds one day in 1883 watching a ball game. He was a metaphysical sort of sports writer, given to weighty speculation, looking for things behind things. On this afternoon he took to studying the posturings of a pitcher, and when the game was over he sat down with his indelible pencil, which wrote purple, and composed the following critique:

> The local pitcher at the Polo Grounds yesterday was, as usual, the object of the most interest. He is

approached in apparent importance only by a big-chested drum-major or the driver of a four-in-hand.

The lordly air that the pitcher exhibited was at once instructive and impressive. After the other men on the field were crouched with their hands on their knees and their eyes riveted on home, the pitcher, with his hat very much over his eyes and his thumb in his belt, would move over to his post before the batter. Once there, he would gaze earnestly at the western sky and gently twirl his finger, assuming an air of total indifference to all.

Meanwhile the batter stood poised with his legs apart, his lips compressed, and his eyes resting un-easily on the indifferent-looking pitcher, while he swung his bat warily.

After a tantalizing wait, the pitcher would turn his eyes casually toward the expectant batter, backed by the anxious catcher and the vigilant umpire. Then, with a twist that would nearly lift him from the ground, he would draw back his arm like a flash and send the ball rushing toward the batter like a bullet from a gun.

When the batter was hit by the ball, as was the case in three instances, the pitcher always ran up kindly and apologized with great good fellowship, while the ladies waved their handkerchiefs and looked sympathetic.

IN THE SOUTHWEST there is a magnificent hotel, owning everything in the way of modern equipment. The manager of this institution is a man who is wedded to his job—he loves everything about the hotel business except the fact that he has to put up with guests. "If there was only some way," he once complained to a friend, "that I could run a hotel without guests, then I'd be happy."

Similarly, there are many umpires who love their work except for one or two small features of it. Paraphrasing the hotel manager, they might say, "If there was only some way of umpiring baseball without a soul in the stands, then I'd be happy—that is, if there were no ballplayers on the field and no managers in the dugouts."

Years ago there was an umpire in the minors named Patrick Shaner who developed what he called a "fan-control system." When the spectators began abusing him for his decisions at the plate, he'd call time, walk into the stands, find a seat there, and yell, "Play ball!" When the next pitch was thrown, Patrick would turn to some fan and say, "What do you say it was—a ball or a strike?" The fan usually would reply, "I wouldn't say for sure—we're pretty far away." And Patrick would conclude, "You are *so* right. Now I'll go back to my regular place of business." He said the stunt, after several repetitions, did a lot toward holding down abuse from the spectators.

Ping Bodie, once an outfielder in the American League, turned umpire and took the incessant carping from the stands until he got sick of it. One afternoon when the spectators were howling against every call he made, he too called time and went into the stands. Settling into a seat, he announced in a loud voice:

"Apparently you folks up here can see what's goin' on down at the plate better than I can when I'm standin' down there. If that's the case, then the proper spot for me is up here, and here I am, and here I stay. *Play ball!*"

And be-dogged if he didn't umpire the rest of the game from that grandstand seat—without so much as a critical whisper from the customers.

JACKSON, the capital city of Mississippi, has been described as a town where nothing much ever happens, where the citizens lead placid and orderly lives. A man from Mars (New York City) checked in at a Jackson hotel on August 15, 1941. He took a shower and had a couple of hookers of tap water and then wandered out to see what he could see. The streets were clean and the buildings were neat and the people were quietly pleasant. There was no sign of any frenzied behavior and even the auto horns seemed to sound subdued.

The visitor from New York heard that there was going to be a good ball game that evening, with Jackson meeting Montgomery, so he made his way to the park and took a seat in the stands. Somehow he had the feeling that the ball game would be a restful and soothing experience, matching the mood of the easygoing town.

First thing that happened, five ballplayers walked onto the field and the announcer described them as expectant fathers. Five tables, each with a large doll on it, were now placed near home plate, and the ballplayers engaged in a wild and noisy diaper-pinning contest.

As soon as that was over, a couple of workmen began digging up the ground near home plate. They worked furiously and as they dug deeper and deeper, two more men appeared carrying a pine casket. The New Yorker figured this was to be a symbolical ceremony—the Jackson team, perhaps, burying the pennant chances of the Montgomery team. He was wrong.

When the grave had been dug, out came a dark-skinned man with a large turban on his head and a robe that a wrestler would have envied. This, said the loud-speakers, was the great Ali Pasha.

Ali Pasha uttered some double-talk prayers, salaamed this way and that, then climbed into the casket. The lid was nailed on, the box was lowered into the grave, and the workmen quickly filled up the hole, tamping the dirt down level and running a heavy roller across it. Following which an umpire marched to the plate and cried, "Play ball!"

Fortunately there were knowing fans in the vicinity of the visitor from New York, and from their conversation he learned that Ali Pasha had contracted to remain buried alive near home plate until the last out of the game was made. One skeptic remarked that Ali Pasha wasn't Ali Pasha at all, but that he was just a colored fellow named William Holley.

"Don't make any difference who he is," argued another man. "He's six foot under, and I didn't see no breathin' tube."

Jackson scored four runs in the first inning, and three runs in the second—meaning that those were especially long innings. From then on the game dragged along at a slow pace, and people took to watching the spot where Ali was buried. "Wouldn't supprise me none," said a spectator, "if he broke outa that box and come outa the ground with the dirt a-flyin'." But he didn't. Two hours elapsed with the game still in the eighth inning and then a hysterical woman leaped from her seat and started yelling, "Dig 'im up!" She turned out to be Mrs. Ali. Nobody made a move with a shovel.

Finally the last out was recorded and the workmen ambled out to the grave and began digging. It took quite a while for

them to get the box uncovered and to drag it out of the grave. Then they stood it up on end, and pried off the lid, and there stood Ali Pasha—on his head. The box was upside down. Ali simply fell out of it, got to his feet and walked slowly off the field while the crowd cheered.

The New Yorker returned to his hotel and went to bed. The next morning, checking out, he was discussing the remarkable feat of Ali Pasha with the desk clerk, and a thought occurred to him.

"By the way," he asked, "who the hell won that ball game?"

"We did," said the clerk.

WHEN HANK GOWDY was coaching for the Cincinnati Reds back in the early 1940s, you didn't need to ask him after a game which team had been the winner. Gowdy had a peculiar habit. Whenever Cincinnati won a game, he immediately ate a large raw onion.

In 1943 Hans Lobert took Gowdy's place on the Reds' coaching staff. A sports writer asked him if he intended carrying on the tradition, if he too would eat a raw onion after each victory. "Never," said Hans. "I don't like onions. Wouldn't eat one if we win six games in a single day."

Just for the record, the Reds won 109 games on their home grounds in the three years that Gowdy was eating onions in their behalf. They won 93 games in the two years that Lobert was scorning onions. This figures out in favor of Lobert, or a no-onion policy.

HEINIE ZIMMERMAN, who achieved great fame as third baseman for the Chicago Cubs many years ago, carried on a one-man war against all umpires. It was said that if an umpire stooped to tie his shoelaces Heinie would descend upon him, accusing him of fraud, corruption, double-dealing, bad eyesight, and secret wagering on the outcome of the game.

One day in 1913 Heinie got a letter which contained one half of a hundred-dollar bill and a note promising that he would receive the other half if he succeeded in restraining his anger against umpires for two weeks. He would collect, the note said, if he went two weeks without once being thrown out of a game. Naturally Heinie figured it was worth a try.

At the end of the stipulated period, he was called to the plate just before the start of a game with Cincinnati. Umpire Brennan handed him an envelope containing the other half of the bill.

At first it was rumored that the umpires themselves had put up the money, figuring it was worth $100 to be free of Zimmerman rhubarbs for a fortnight. They denied it. Next it was reported that C. W. Murphy, owner of the Cubs, engineered the stunt as a means of keeping his star infielder on the playing field. He denied it. Finally word got out that a Chicago newspaper was responsible.

Two weeks of this self-discipline, you may think, caused Heinie to modify his manner toward umpires. It did not. He stayed in the National League for five or six years after that, and never once overlooked an opportunity to scorch an umpire.

THE CHIPPED ELBOW, the Charley horse, the separated shoulder, and the calcification are physiological matters familiar to modern baseball fans. Among the more unusual injuries sustained by ballplayers have been the following:

Frenchy Bordagaray hurt his leg when he fell off the bench during an exciting moment in a game at Ebbets Field.

George Case was laid up after he injured his shoulder getting into his overcoat.

Bernie Neis grabbed a cake of soap into which his roommate had stuck a razor blade for safekeeping; consequence—a bad gash on the hand.

Freddie Fitzsimmons was rocking back and forth, lazily, in a rocking chair on the porch of a hotel at training camp. His arm was dangling over the side of the chair and Freddie managed to rock over his fingers. Couldn't pitch for a while.

Frank Crosetti injured the ligaments of his leg climbing into an upper berth.

Bill Werber broke a toe when, in anger, he kicked a water bucket.

Whitey Moore stumbled over a photographer's camera, snatched it up, threw it into a concrete wall, and was cut on the face by bits of glass that bounced back.

George Metkovich had to go to a hospital after his foot had been pierced by the fin of a huge catfish. George was wearing sneakers and put his foot on the fish while extracting the hook.

SEVERAL YEARS AGO when Eddie Basinski was an infielder for the Brooklyn Dodgers he was approached by one of his teammates.

"Eddie," said the teammate, "some of the boys have been makin' some bets about you. It got around that you are a fiddle player in the off season. Several of the boys don't believe it—especially the story that you play high-class and not hillbilly. So some bets have been made and you got to settle it by bringing your fiddle out and playing some."

Eddie had to write home to Lancaster, New York, to have his violin sent down. It arrived at Ebbets Field late one afternoon just before the Dodgers assembled for a night game. Eddie unpacked it, called the boys around him, and began playing a concert in the finest classical tradition.

Those who had wagered that Eddie could play the violin now demanded their money. But some of the players who had taken the opposite view—especially those from the West—put up a stout argument.

"If," said their spokesman, "if that's fiddle playin', then I'm a suck-aig mule. We're not payin' off till we hear him play 'Turkey in th' Straw.'"

The cultural argument raged and then was arbitrated. A sports writer was called in to listen and decide, from the sounds made by Eddie, if he actually *was* playing the violin. The sports writer already knew that Mr. Basinski not only was a capable concert violinist but had played with the Buffalo Philharmonic Orchestra. So he ruled against the hillbilly element, and the losers grudgingly paid off.

Music, it turned out, hath charms to confuse the savage Brooks. After that classical concert, the Dodgers took the field against the Cardinals, who slaughtered them 15 to 3.

DESPERATE MANAGERS sometimes use desperate measures. The Duluth team of the Northern League got off to a horrible start in the first two weeks of the 1947 season. After losing seven straight games Manager Paul Bowa was in a state. He went home and paced the floor, growling at the furniture, kicking the cat, and finally he said to Mrs. Bowa: "You're going to be vice-president in charge of the line-up for tomorrow's game." He gave her the list of players and she fussed around with it, and finally handed him her idea of a proper batting order. The sequence was one he'd never have dreamed of using, and he told himself that it was crazy, but he went through with it. His team won the next day. The day after that they won both ends of a double-header. And they went on to finish fourth in the standings.

When Billy Herman was managing the Pittsburgh Pirates, also in 1947, he tried a similar stunt. His team was just a shade out of the cellar and things were going from bad to worse. So Herman asked a Pittsburgh sports writer to jigger his line-up around. The scribe took him at his word. He pulled Hank Greenberg off first base, lifted the shortstop from seventh position in the batting order to leadoff, shifted the outfielders around, and performed other startling alterations. With this new setup the Pirates beat the Dodgers 16 to 3, but lost the next two games to the Phillies and, after that, Herman decided it was time to go back to his own system.

COULD IT BE that we of the atomic-bomb era are less genteel than the people who lived in the time of the Gatling gun? A New York newspaper had some editorial comment to make one day back in 1862 regarding the conduct of C. Bomeisler, an outfielder for Philadelphia during a game with Brooklyn. Said the paper:

"We have to comment in terms anything but praiseworthy on the actions of C. Bomeisler, especially when he tried to irritate the opposing catcher in the last inning by chafing him.

"We trust he will never again be the means of marring the harmony of a match as he was in this game. Every player in a match renders himself amenable to public comment, the mantle of privacy being thrown off on all such occasions."

One thing is certain: editorial writers ain't changed much at all.

THE CINCINNATI *ENQUIRER* was famous among newspapermen for years because of the bizarre heads appearing over its stories. The following sample appeared back in the days when the celebrated Tim Hurst was umpiring:

BANG!

Right at His Head

The Beer Glass Was Thrown.

Tim Hurst Lets His Quick Temper

Get the Best of Him and Trouble Follows.

Almost a Tragedy at the Cincinnati Park.

Pittsburg Got a Dose of Its Own Medicine—Jesse James's Tactics All Around.

The party who dug that head up for us didn't furnish any further details, possibly because they are not really needed.

WE ARE PROUD to present, herewith, a success story. Our hero is six feet tall, twenty-one years old, works on a farm, and pitches like a champion. His name is Bennett Mitchell.

Six days a week he works in the peanut and tobacco fields. On Sundays, in season, he pitches for a semipro team at Jarratt, down in Virginia.

Early in the season of 1948 Bennett pitched two no-hit games. In one of those contests no opposing player reached first base.

News of that kind of pitching gets around and soon the major-league scouts were Virginia-bound.

First came Percy Dawson of the Yankees. Later on George Selkirk of the Yankee organization also visited the young farmer. Ossie Bluege of the Washington Senators and Bill Harris of the New York Giants turned up in Jarratt. Scouts from the Athletics, the Dodgers, and Pirates came to have a look.

All of these city fellers brought documents which they waved before Bennett Mitchell. They talked fast and pretty—told him about all the money that would be his if he signed; and the glamour that goes with being a big-league pitcher; and how he'd probably have his picture in *Life,* maybe even on the front; and how he'd be on television shows and people would swarm round him for autographs, and all that. To each of these the young man replied:

"Sorry. Can't oblige you. My dad's sick and somebody's got to work the farm."

And working the farm is what he's doing today—with occasional pitching assignments on Sundays.

MR. RALPH BETTS of Cumberland, Maryland, a devout follower of the Pittsburgh Pirates, took a look one morning at the National League standings and groaned. The Pirates were in seventh place and Mr. Betts was unhappy. Remote from the scenes of battle though he was, he still felt there was something he could do to help. He began thinking in terms of some talisman that might bring a change of luck; the one thing on earth, he decided, that everybody seemed to think was designed by Mother Nature as a good-luck charm was the four-leaf clover. So Mr. Betts went scrabbling around for some of this freak greenery. Just where he got them is not clear, but he collected ninety-three clovers carrying a total of 372 leaves. He packaged them carefully and sent them on to the Pirates. The day after they arrived Pittsburgh plunged into the National League cellar.

MANAGING the New Orleans club one hot afternoon, Ray Blades, the former Cardinal, lost his temper over an umpire's decision. Mr. Blades began giving the umpire the ragged edge of his tongue. After a while the ump got tough, and told Mr. Blades that if he said one more word he would be thrown out of the game and fined. Mr. Blades had been contending that the umpire's decision was directly contrary to the law of the game as stated in the official rule book, but now he was gagged. Forbidden to talk, he dug up a copy of the rule book, tore out the page on which the rule in question was printed. Then, the next time he went to the coaching box, he managed to walk close by the umpire and ram the loose page into the official's coat pocket. Didn't say a word, either.

A MAN NAMED Cash-and-Carry Pyle promoted a cross-country bunion derby twenty-odd years ago, gaining national celebrity for it. Years later another man named Pyle acquired a degree of local celebrity in Meridian, Mississippi, for taking a long walk.

This Pyle, first-named Mervin, was the type of fan who gets sore at his ball team when the team is guilty of ragged play. Such fans, and they are legion, are usually the most vociferous in the abuse they heap upon their favorite ballplayers. As Dizzy Dean might put it, they holler disgustilly.

So here was Mr. Pyle in the stands, and Meridian batting in the last of the ninth with the score tied. The more loyal Meridian fans had been eying Mr. Pyle with extreme disfavor for several innings, in view of his sarcastic remarks about the quality of the fielding. Now the home team's top hitter, Hal Summers, stepped to the plate, and a spectator seated near Mr. Pyle cried:

"Bust 'er one for a home run, Hal!"

"Ha!" roared Mr. Pyle with deep sarcasm. "That's a good one! Fat chance that bum's got of hittin' a home run! He hits a home run, I'll walk all the way home barefooted!"

The words had scarcely passed his lips when Hal Summers bradded one into the faraway. And now Mr. Pyle was surrounded by fans. He must pay his debt to society. Society was going to see to it that he did pay. They stood by while he took off his shoes and socks, and they walked in a large group with him, all the way home.

TWO IMPORTANT MEN chanced to meet one day in St. Louis. One was Fred M. Vinson, Chief Justice of the United States Supreme Court. The other was Beans Reardon, veteran umpire in the National League.

"I've got the edge on you," said Mr. Reardon to the chief justice. "All I've got to do is think what my decision is and then say what it is. You've got to have some other fellows voting with you in order to make a decision."

"There's much to what you say," agreed the chief justice, "but you must remember one thing. I can go out to the ball park and boo your decisions, but you can't take a seat in the Supreme Court chamber and boo a decision there."

HARRY COVELESKIE died in August of 1950 at Shamokin, Pennsylvania. He is still called "The Giant Killer" because of some sweet pitching he did back in 1908. He was with the Phillies, and he really foxed up the Giants that year. The New Yorkers were all but a sure thing to win the pennant and then, along toward the close of the regular season, young Harry mowed them down three times in a row—whipping the great Mathewson in the bargain. He forced them into a playoff with the Cubs, and the Cubs won the pennant.

Convinced that this one man had deprived them of the league championship, the Giants yearned for a chance to get revenge. A year passed before they stumbled upon a gimmick they could use against the young man from Pennsylvania.

One of the Giant players lived near Coveleskie's home town,

Shamokin. He had news for his teammates when he arrived for the beginning of the 1909 season. Coveleskie, he said, had spent the winter courting a young lady in Shamokin. Everybody in town knew about it. The love-smitten pitcher would station himself near the girl's house of an evening and warble chorus after chorus of "Sweet Adeline." He was a better pitcher than he was a singer, and the informant said that even the neighborhood cats took to singing back at him.

That was all the Giants needed. The first time Coveleskie faced them in the new season, they let matters proceed for a few innings and then they began one of the most skillful heckling campaigns in the history of baseball. In the dugout the Giants' choral group would boom out with "Sweet Adeline" and, at the conclusion of the singing, the Giant coaches, off first and third, would cry out in tones of anguish, such remarks as, "Oh, dearie, will you be mine?" Over and over again the Giants wailed their lament to Harry, and Harry grew wild and the batters got to him.

Word quickly spread around the league that Coveleskie could be had and now, no matter where he pitched, the songsters bellowed in the dugouts, the coaches cried out in lovesick accents, and Harry grew wilder and wilder. Sports writers said that this form of persecution soon forced him out of the league altogether.

It needs to be added that the young Pennsylvanian (brother of the celebrated Stanley Coveleskie) returned to the majors after an interlude of three or four years, this time with the Detroit Tigers. By this time his weakness had been forgotten—either that or American Leaguers are more gentlemanly than National Leaguers—and he had several years of successful pitching before he retired in 1919. He had a lifetime record of eighty-four victories and fifty-four defeats. The records are woefully incomplete, since they fail to show how many of those defeats were brought about by the singing of "Sweet Adeline."

ROWLAND HIGH SCHOOL was defeated by the Lumberton High School nine at Lumberton, North Carolina, by a score of 6 to 0 one day in May of 1929. The Rowland High players failed to get a hit off the star pitcher for Lumberton, Richard Norment. In fact, Richard had, just two weeks earlier, pitched a two-hitter against Clarkton High.

Richard was nineteen and pitched that kind of baseball though he had only one arm and one leg—the consequence of a railroad wreck when he was eight years old.

THE DEFENDANT at the bar was James Key. On the bench was Judge Christopher Stein. Key was accused of creating a disturbance at the Detroit ball park by running onto the playing field during a game between the Tigers and the Red Sox.

Mr. Key had been in the stands, watching the Red Sox wallop the Tigers, brooding over the clumsiness of some of the Detroit players, and in particular the inept performance of Hoot Evers in center field. Finally he just went over the fence, dashed out to center field, and yelled at Evers: "Go somewhere and take a rest and let somebody play center field that knows how to play center field!"

Judge Stein said it was a bad thing to have done and imposed a fine of five dollars. Then he added:

"You did wrong, but I must admit that I've sometimes been tempted to do the same thing."

The ball once struck off,
Away flies the boy
To the next destined post,
And then home with joy.

The above poem isn't much. It's scarcely worth memorizing. We insert it here, however, for the reason that it is described in H. L. Mencken's *New Dictionary of Quotations* as possibly the first printed reference to the game of baseball. It appeared in 1744 in a volume called *A Little Pretty Pocketbook*. Very interesting, considering that baseball wasn't invented until about a hundred years later.

BASEBALL REFORMERS with radical notions pop up from time to time and one of these in recent years was Dr. A. R. Oestricher, of Orlando, Florida. The doctor diagnosed "a dry rot that is creeping into the game both on the playing field and at the gate." He had, also, a cure.

"I suggest," he said, "that every year the clubs finishing last in each major league be replaced the following season by the pennant winners of the International League and American Association.

"There is little question that the winning teams in these Class AA leagues play a far better brand of baseball than the chronic major-league tail-enders.

"If this plan were adopted I believe baseball would profit greatly. Attendance would increase in both the major and minor leagues as a result of the keener competition and there would be no loafing on the field."

MEMBERS of the Houston club of the Texas League, all men with fairly rough necks, were aboard a train one day in 1908 starting their first road trip of the new season. The train was less than a dozen miles out of Houston when a woman carrying a baby got up from her coach seat and approached a pitcher named W. E. Hester, who was seated across the aisle.

"Would you mind," she asked, "holding the baby for a few minutes?"

Hester was not a man with any strong inclinations to hold babies and he made a feeble effort to avoid it. "Do you want it helt left-handed or right-handed?" he asked, figuring that if she said left-handed he'd beg off on the grounds that he was a right-hander, and vice versa. But she said it didn't make a bit of difference, and there he was with a baby in his lap.

The mother disappeared from the car, and when she hadn't returned in half an hour, Hester called the conductor and asked some questions. The woman had alighted from the train 'way back yonder, and Hester was stuck with the infant. He now summoned several of his teammates, thinking they would be able to help him stow the kid somewhere, but all they did was sit around and poke the infant in the stomach and say "Google-google" and "gitchee-gitchee." The ballplayers, in fact, took a strong liking for the kid and one of them suggested: "If its mama don't show up, le's us keep it and grow it up." The idea met with majority approval and when the train reached Dallas, the ballplayers marched in an enthusiastic body to a restaurant and ordered pork chops and fried potatoes for their new mascot. By good fortune a waiter in the place, who had a cousin who had once had a small baby, set them right on the matter of infant diet.

There was considerable in the way of newspaper publicity about the ballplayers' baby and the fans were deeply impressed. In Dallas, Fort Worth, and other cities of the circuit, the Houston players took the baby to the ball games and before the start of each contest, they would alternate carrying the child onto the field and exhibiting it to the spectators. Then there would be a brief speech, and the hat would be passed, and in a very short time a fund of more than $2,000 had been raised.

Some fans, of course, tried to turn this situation back on the Houston team. They'd show up at the ball park sucking on pacifiers and shaking rattles and waving diapers and yelling "Wa-a-a-a-aaaaa!" Several of these got their teeth scattered.

By the time they got home from their road trip, the players had learned that they couldn't go on hauling the baby around the circuit, jouncing it around on the bench, housing it in assorted fleabags. The law wouldn't permit it. So the team's third baseman, Roy Akin, went to court and adopted the child legally, promising that it would enjoy a normal home life in the future.

Contemporary newspaper accounts say that some of the Houston ballplayers didn't know the infant was a male child until the matter had to be specified in the adoption papers. It was recorded that Akin, the adopter, remarked as the papers were being signed: "Wouldn't it be a good one on us if he grew up to be an umpire?"

What did he grow up to be? We don't know. Perhaps one of the Houston newspapers will be able to find out.

THE COMMON EXPRESSION "being in the doghouse" was used only in reference to dogs forty years ago—to dogs and a Philadelphia outfielder

named Socks Seybold. In those far-off days there was a doghouse at the base of the center-field wall in the Washington
ball park. It was not used for dogs. A flag pole stood close beside
it and each evening when the groundkeeper hauled down the
banner, he folded it and placed it in the little house for protec-
tion against the weather. The thing resembled a doghouse
merely by chance. It had been built to house the flag and the
opening was big enough for a man to get his head and shoulders
inside.

Socks Seybold was in center field for the Athletics one afternoon when a Washington player slammed the ball over his
head. It rolled straight to the doghouse and through the opening. Socks arrived on the run and stuck his arm through the
opening and grabbed around a bit without finding the ball. He
got down and peered inside and saw the ball was in a far
corner. So in went Socks's head and shoulders. He measured a
good ax handle across the shoulders, whereas the groundkeeper
was a lean man. Socks got in, all right, but when he tried to

back out he couldn't make it. Thousands of spectators could see
nothing but his big stern, threshing around madly, as the

Washington batter circled the bases and returned to the bench. He could have gone around again before Socks finally jerked himself free, considerably skinned up and considerably profane.

THE FOLLOWING appeared in the New York *Times* in 1915:

A NEW BASEBALL SCHEME

Managers of both major and minor league teams who believe their men are not playing their best might use a bonus scheme, advanced by an expert of the diamond. There are many reasons why a baseball player might not put his heart into his work. One is the inability of a strange player to associate amicably with his teammates. Old men may be jealous of a newcomer, his ability or his salary.

It is a general complaint that the stars are not giving the best in them, while the young players, outbatting and outfielding their veteran teammates, are dissatisfied because they are tied by contracts calling for only one-third or one-half of the salary of the older players.

A part bonus and part straight salary system in the baseball player's contract would help remedy some of the present injustices of baseball, says an expert who makes these suggestions:

Fix a standard salary of $1,800 or $2,000 a year. Then arrange a bonus system applicable to the various classes of players.

A bonus of $1,000 might go to all pitchers finishing the season with an average of .500 or better; $1,500 bonus money to the men winning 60 per cent of their games; $2,000 bonus money to the men winning two-thirds of their games; $3,000 bonus to the men winning three-fourths of their games, and $4,000 bonus to the men who finish the season with a mark of .750 or better. Thus a pitcher would be paid for what he did during the current season, and not for what he has done in other seasons.

Outfielders, infielders and catchers might be guaranteed $2,000 a year. They would earn their bonuses by good fielding and batting. This is a suggested schedule of bonuses for batting:

.241 to .250	$ 250
.251 to .260	350
.261 to .270	500
.271 to .280	600
.281 to .290	750
.291 to .300	1,000
.301 to .310	1,250
.311 to .320	1,500
.321 to .330	2,000
.331 to .340	2,500
.341 to .350	3,000
Over .350	3,750

There follow two tables of suggested bonus scales for fielding percentages, after which the writer resumes:

A penalty system could be arranged so that a player who batted under a minimum figure or who fielded under a minimum figure would suffer deductions from the bonus earned in the other department. For instance, if a player hit .295 he would be entitled to $1,000 bonus money, but if he fielded only .900 he might lose $250 from his other bonus.

If a player earned no bonuses, and hit and fielded below the minimum, no deductions would be made, for the $2,000 straight salary would be inviolate. With the bonus system in operation, an infielder who batted .325 and fielded .965 would get $2,000 bonus for batting and $1,000 bonus for fielding, making a total of $5,000.

AT HAND is a yellow-backed booklet, published in 1910 and bearing the title: *On the Road with the Base Ball Bugs*. The authors are Jack Regan and Will E. Stahl, and the contents consist of jokes and jingles. In all your born days you never saw such corn.

Included in the booklet, however, is a parody which deserves the attention of such baseball fans as there are in the world who happen also to be Shakespeare fans. It is titled *The Batter's Soliloquy*, its author is Donald Douglass, and it is prefaced with a line stating that it deals with a situation in the ninth inning, man on third, two out and the score tied at 2–2. The soliloquy itself follows:

> *To wait, or not to wait,—that is the question:*
> *Whether 'tis nobler in this game to suffer*

The taunts and yells of the outrageous fans,
Or dodge the curves and drops of an erratic pitcher,
And, by my coolness, 'scape them? To wait—to walk,—
No more; and by a walk to say we stroll
To first, and then be daring like Ty Cobb,
And work the Double Steal,—'tis a consummation
Devoutly to be wished. To walk—to steal—
To steal. Perchance to score. Ay, there's the rub;—
For in that Double Steal what chance may come
When we have rattled the opposing pitcher,
Must give us runs; there's the respect
That makes a walk of so long life;
For who would bear the yells and taunts of fans,
The umpire's wrong, the bleachers' contumely,

The *pangs of disprized hope, the game's delay,*
The insolence of gamins, and the spurns
That one must take from the unknowing
When he himself his fame might make
By a 2-bagger? Who would roastings bear,
To grunt and swear under a weary game,
But that the dread of something after it,
The Minor Leagues, from whose ranks
No old time star returns, startles the mind;
And makes us rather bear those ills we have
Then fly to others whence we ne'er return?
These bleachers do make cowards of us all;
And thus the fumble of a hard-hit grounder,
Is yelled at by the bleacher mob,
And, thus in places of great chance and moment,
We all make bone-head plays that lose the game.

THE SEAL of a government department is displayed on each of the automobiles assigned to high federal officials in Washington. And what's that got to do with baseball? To get the answer, we must go back to Teddy Roosevelt's time.

In those days, as now, members of Congress and high officials in the executive branch of government sometimes slipped away from their jobs and went out to see the Washington team play. Among the most regular customers at the ball park was a young man connected with one of the executive departments. Members of Congress got their share of attention from the other fans, but this fellow always made a big splash. He came in a fancy trap drawn by a pair of beautiful horses and he always drove his rig to a spot where the left-field foul line met the fence. The customers couldn't watch the game without being aware of his elegance.

Some of the congressional fans didn't like it. To be truthful, they were envious, because they traveled to the ball park in hacks or streetcars and had to sit in the grandstand. So one of them, an important man in the House of Representatives, decided he'd put a crimp in the stylish behavior of the young undersecretary. He introduced legislation demanding that every government vehicle bear the insignia of the department to which it belonged, and that the insignia be displayed prominently on the vehicle. He believed that the flashy young man, forced to advertise the fact that he was playing hooky from his department, would change his ways.

As soon as the law went into effect the young man in question had the seal of his department painted underneath his conveyance, on the axle facing toward the horses. Within a few days he was challenged by the legislator responsible for the new law.

"Saw you out at the game yesterday," said the congressman, "and you haven't got the seal painted on your rig."

"Oh yes I have," said the young man.

"Where?"

"Well," said the young man, "if you'll crouch down, right alongside the rear ends of the two horses, which is your rightful place, you'll be able to see it painted on the axle."

For some reason the congressman was infuriated by this remark, and went to work with the intention of having the whippersnapper canned out of the government; he was frustrated, however, by the fact that the rig was not government property, but belonged to the young man.

The law stayed on the books and there it is today—a monument to the fancy ways and congressman-baiting turn of a man who sits around the National Press Club of afternoons and recalls the good old days.

THERE HAVE BEEN many cases of dogs getting loose in baseball parks and causing confusion. At Minneapolis around 1945 a pair of dogs sometimes got into the action on what might be called a semiofficial basis. These dogs, two Dalmatians, were the property of Mike Kelly, owner of the Minneapolis club, and Mr. Kelly pursued the practice of stationing himself and his animals in the right-field corner of the park during games. The Dalmatians were content to watch the game save when a ball came in their direction and then they'd sometimes get excited. It is understood that Kelly and his dogs finally yielded to pressure, largely from the rival Milwaukee players, and removed themselves from fair ground. On one occasion a Milwaukee player hit a line drive toward the corner, and Herb Barna, the Minneapolis right fielder, chased after it. So did one of the Dalmatians. Barna reached the ball first and started to pick it up, and the dog tried to remove his hand at the wrist. The Milwaukee batter made it to second but the umpire ordered him back to first, ruling that there had been beastly interference.

Kelly's two dogs guarded the clubhouse at night. One of them had been stone-deaf from birth. Burglars got into the clubhouse while the dogs were on guard and, in the melee that followed, one of the thieves picked up a bat and walloped the deaf dog on the head. That dog had good hearing thereafter.

HERSCHEL LYONS, pitcher for Sacramento in 1942, had trouble with a dog during a game with San Francisco. The dog, a yellow mongrel, came on the playing field the moment the game started. He brought on interruptions several times and during one of the early innings forty ballplayers and two umpires were racing around in a pack, trying to catch him. Along about the sixth inning, having rested himself near the outfield wall, the dog came bounding back toward the infield. This time Pitcher Lyons grabbed him, near second base. The animal had no collar on and Lyons was determined to get him the hell out of the park, so he removed his belt, fastened it around the dog's neck, and started leading him toward the dugout. Halfway there Herschel's pants suddenly fell down around his ankles, in full view of the crowd. He said later he was tempted, at that point when the fans were roaring with laughter, to kick the dog half to death, but he suppressed the urge, pulled up his pants and held them in place, and escorted the invader to the door.

TEN YEARS AGO a citizen of Youngstown, Ohio, snagged a foul rabbit for a souvenir one day during a game between the local team and the St. Louis Browns—a pre-season exhibition match. The rabbit appeared on the field during the fifth inning and play was halted. As in the case with most zoological visitors to ball games, the rabbit didn't want to leave, and didn't want human hands laid on him. So minor-league and major-league ballplayers, plus an umpire and a bat boy, chased him back and forth and around and around. Jack Kramer and Roy Cullenbine were closing in on him at last when the rabbit gave a mighty leap, landing in a knot of customers in the grandstand. There a man made a nice one-handed catch, and the disturbance was over. The customer, of course, got to keep the rabbit.

RICHMOND was playing Charlotte at Charlotte in 1941. In the ninth Bob Ortiz, the Charlotte right fielder, hit a long drive, and as he rounded first, a small dog hove in view. The dog went after Ortiz, caught up with him, and scampered along beside him on his way to second. The runner's cap flew off near second, the dog snatched it from the ground and began playing with it, and Ortiz went on into third with a triple. Later he scored the winning run, after the cap had been removed from the dog and the dog from the field. The next day a Charlotte newspaper carried these lines at the bottom of the box score:

> x—Nix batted for Pritchard in ninth.
> y—Dog ran with Ortiz in ninth.
> z—Two out when winning run was
> scored.

ASSUMING that no sports writer would ever be guilty of exaggeration, let us consider the published report of a ball game at Battle Creek a dozen years ago. A dog came racing onto the field, ducked behind the pitcher's mound, and grabbed the resin bag. The pitcher tried to coax it away from him, but the dog stayed out of reach. The pitcher then thought if he'd offer the dog his glove, the animal would drop the tasty resin bag. The dog accepted the offer, dropped the bag, seized the glove and made off with it. After a delay of six minutes the pitcher managed to snatch his glove back and the dog was chased off the field. He remained away

until the seventh inning when a particular sequence of events excited his interest. A batter had just hit a line drive and was running hard, rounding first and trying for a double. The dog took off after the runner, caught him midway to second, leaped for him and seized him by the seat of the pants. With a dog fastened to his behind, the runner went into a long slide, throwing his body sideways. The second baseman, the ball, and the runner with dog attached all arrived at the second sack at approximately the same instant. The umpire ruled the runner was safe. The second baseman, pivoting to make the tag, was just a trifle late, and tagged the dog.

THE WITCHERY associated with black cats has been brought to bear in the sport of baseball from time to time, with questionable consequences. Some members of the St. Louis Cardinals swore that a black cat won a game for them back in 1941 at their home park. They were playing the Dodgers, and in the third inning, with no score, Max Lanier walked three Brooklyn men to fill the bases with two out. Mickey Owen was the next Brooklyn batter and was on his way up to the plate, grimly determined to fetch in some runs. At that moment a black cat came streaking in from center field, circled home plate and then headed down the right-field foul line. Enos Slaughter was in right field but he made no effort to chase the cat. The animal finally sat down, just outside the foul line, and gazed in toward the plate. Play was resumed. Lanier pitched to Owen. Owen hit an easy grounder straight to Marty Marion, who threw to first for the third out. The Cardinals won the game, 1 to 0.

ONE DAY in April of 1936 Ernie Smith, of the Fort Worth club, was sitting in the lobby of a San Antonio hotel, grieving over the low condition into which his team had fallen. Twelve losses in a row! Something had to be done. Ernie put his reasoning powers to work. If you were having a lot of bad luck, he thought, maybe something that's supposed to bring you *bad* luck would actually bring you *good* luck. A black cat, for instance. He got up and made his way to a pet store where by chance they had a black cat. They wanted twenty-five dollars for it, but Ernie figured that was a little steep. He wandered around town and finally came upon a little girl with a black cat. He made a deal with her—bought the cat for all the change he had in his pocket, totaling $2.35. That afternoon the cat was tethered to the Fort Worth bench and Fort Worth scored two runs in the top of the ninth to take the lead and win the game from San Antonio.

COLUMBUS and Augusta of the South Atlantic League were playing one afternoon in the early forties. The Columbus pitcher was in a jam. He had just walked one man on four straight pitches, and now had thrown three wide ones to the next batter. At this point a black cat came skedaddling in from the neighborhood of first base and crossed the diamond diagonally toward third, passing between the pitcher and the batter. Time was called for a few minutes and there was much speculation among players and fans. A black cat had crossed somebody's path, but whose? Was he hexing the pitcher or the batter? There was only one way to find out—continue the game. The batter fouled out to the catcher on the next pitch.

SEVERAL YOUNG MEN spent the morning of July 26, 1940, scouring the town of New Bern, North Carolina, in a search for black cats. That afternoon they were to meet Williamston and they yearned desperately for victory. The New Bern team was in a horrible slump and had tried everything else; now a few of the players decided to try black cats.

They had accumulated six of them by game time. Each of the cats was on a leash, and while the pitchers were warming up, the ballplayers paraded the jinx critters back and forth before the Williamston dugout. The stunt brought a resurgence of spirit and fire and dash to the whole New Bern team. They went onto the field, eager to fight on to victoree.

Williamston won the ball game.

THE PRESIDENT of the United States, man by the name of Hoover, sat down one day in 1929 and wrote a letter to a schoolboy about a possum. The boy was Bob Venemann, member of the ball team at Hyattsville High School in Maryland. He had read about how a possum had been presented to the President for a pet, and he wrote to Mr. Hoover, saying he had heard tell that a possum generally brought good luck to a baseball team. Would the President let the Hyattsville boys borrow that possum for a while? The President replied that he would—to come and get it. So the Hyattsville team, with a possum on its bench, won the county high school championship.

After the possum was returned, with much thanks, the President wrote to Bob Venemann:

"I am glad to have your formal report on the efficiency of Billy O. Possum—it will be incorporated into his service record. Precautions will be taken to maintain his health and spirits for the further needs of your team."

PIGEONS get involved in ball games so frequently that it was a sure thing one of them would some day get his lumps. In a game between the Red Sox and the Athletics at Boston back in 1945, two pigeons arrived over the field and began performing as if they'd been paid. They looped and zoomed and fluttered around the infield, and sailed into the outfield, and no amount of towel-waving or improper language would make them go home. The game proceeded, and Tom McBride, Boston center fielder, went after a long fly ball hit by Sam Chapman in the third. McBride lost sight of the ball temporarily, then got it in focus again, he thought, but it wasn't the ball—it was one of the pigeons flying the same path as the ball. McBride, of course, missed the catch and Chapman got a double. Shortly after that McBride, madder than a wet squab, cooled off considerably. One of the pigeons—he hoped it was that stinker that had fouled him up—got in the way of a ball thrown hard from the outfield. The ball took the bird in mid-air and knocked him to the ground. He looked to be dead, but before anyone could get to him, he struggled up, took to the air in some pain and limped off toward the interior of Massachusetts where contract bridge is the leading sport.

A CRIPPLED PIGEON fluttered into the Indianapolis ball park around Labor Day in 1949. The bird had a broken leg and the Indianapolis trainer put a splint on it and started nursing it back to robust health. The Indianapolis club promptly went on a winning streak and the players attributed it all to the pigeon, now named Podner. The club went into a post-season playoff with Milwaukee. After winning three games, the Indianapolis boys lost two in a row and then figured out what was wrong. They were in Milwaukee and Podner was in Indianapolis. The pigeon was flown up to Milwaukee on a commercial airline, arriving just before game time, and Indianapolis won the game, the series, and the right to meet Montreal in the Little World Series. With Podner on the bench, it was a sure thing now for Indianapolis to win the Series. They did.

SAN FRANCISCO was playing at Sacramento one night in 1947. A San Francisco catcher, loafing in the bull pen, saw a slight movement near the wall, walked over, found a frightened rat, and trapped it in his cap. This catcher, named Ogrodowski, was known to his teammates as a card. He decided to amble into the dugout and release the rat there and scare the britches offa summa them smart rookies. The rat, however, didn't scare the rookies so much as the rookies scared the rat. The critter bounced out of the dugout, ran onto the infield, and began circling and crisscrossing, always staying inside the base lines. Balls were thrown at it. Bats were thrown at it. One player tried to hit it with his shoe. Once when it was dancing around near second, a ballplayer was heard to shout: "What's the plate umparr doin' out at second?" At last the rat disappeared into a corner of the park and play was resumed—the delay was clocked at seven minutes.

THE LARGEST swarm of bees in the history of mankind, or at least in the history of Kentucky, all but broke up a ball game in Louisville one afternoon in the early 1920s. The bees arrived by way of the outfield, pausing to have a look and perhaps a bite of Earle Combs, who was playing his position out there. Combs ran around in circles for a while, then straightened his course and raced for the nearest exit. The dark cloud that followed him finally swerved and went into the grandstand where the fans had been laughing fit to die. Pandemonium followed, quite a few people were stung, and then the bees departed in the direction of Indiana.

YOUNG DEL ENNIS stood at the plate in the eleventh inning of a game between the Giants and the Phillies at Philadelphia on April 26, 1949. The Giants had scored twice in the top of the eleventh to break the tie and lead 11 to 9. Now in the last half of the inning the Phillies had got one man across, had another on base, and here, as mentioned, stood Del Ennis. Suddenly he let out a yelp and clapped his hand to his neck, and there was a delay. A bee had stung him. After a few moments he stepped back in the box and now *he* stung the pitcher—for a home run that won the game.

ONE DAY an unsolicited white rabbit arrived by express at the Detroit ball park. Attached was the following note:

> *Bunny Bill is an abundance of luck and tough as a tiger. He was born at Manhattan Beach, California, March 1st. He has chewed up a chow dog and bitten a man. Besides dogs and men, he eats rabbit pelts, bananas, lettuce, tomatoes, hard tack, cantaloupe, raw potatoes, celery, carrots and vegetable tops. Be good to him and he will bring you luck for many years.*

He did too, sorta.

IN THE DISTANT ERA of 1935 the Philadelphia Phillies were doing better than usual in the National League because, they believed, of their mascot—a little white rabbit. Along about June of that year the Cardinals came in to Philadelphia for a series with Dizzy Dean scheduled to pitch the opener. Before the game Dizzy heard about the white rabbit and wandered over to the enemy dugout to have a look at it. He cooed at it and rubbed its back and then went out and won himself a ball game.

The next time the Cardinals came in, Dizzy was again scheduled to pitch. He went immediately to the Phillies' dugout and rubbed the rabbit, and won the game.

He figured that now he had a cinch in all future engagements with the Phillies—but the rabbit died. And the Philadelphia team gave it a proper burial, beneath a marker inscribed:

HERE DIZZY DEAN'S LUCK LIES BURIED

OF ALL the zoological adventures among ballplayers, one of the most unusual was that experienced by Ray Villeneuve, a seventeen-year-old outfielder for St. Michael's High School. Playing at Hatfield, Massachusetts, one day in 1950, Ray went after a long high foul. Before he could get to it a horse rushed up and bit him. It wasn't a bad bite, as horse bites go, and Ray was able to continue in the game after first-aid treatment.

DONALD ATKINSON, umpiring several years ago in the Georgia-Florida League, had a habit of discarding his coat on hot days and using a canvas bag slung over his shoulder for the storage of spare baseballs. As with other umpires, it was his custom when a new ball was needed to reach for it and throw it quickly to the pitcher. One afternoon he reached and threw, but not to the pitcher. He threw in the direction he happened to be facing at the moment —down the first base line, and a loud yell preceded the peg. Some pixy had slipped a fat toad-frog into the bag and that was what Donald had grabbed. It was one of the longest throws in Georgia-Florida history, at least one of the longest ever made with a toad-frog.

SOME YEARS AGO Jim Lawrence was manager of the Lake Charles club in the Evangeline League. Jim had a rather strange custom. He kept a live horned toad in his cap during every ball game—in his cap while he was wearing it. Most people assumed the thing was a good-luck token, but when Jim was questioned about it, he denied it, and said he wasn't superstitious. "I keep it in my cap," he said, "because it feels good."

THERE WERE toads all over the ball park at Gainesville, Florida, during one season about ten years ago. The groundkeeper was having trouble with pests—he figured they were mole crickets—which were damaging his turf. He had heard that toads are great at destroying mole crickets and he figured out a way to get toads. He made a deal with the proprietor of a local movie house, who was a baseball fan. The theater advertised that every kid who arrived with a toad would be admitted free. Barrels of toads resulted, and the playing field was saved.

AND FINALLY, in this zoological section, a chicken. Roger Cramer, playing center field for Detroit in a game at Comiskey Park in 1945, saw a red hen crossing between his position and second base. Roger caught it and found a card tied to it. The card said: "This is to be a gift for the winning pitcher." Three Detroit pitchers laid eggs, but Earl Caldwell pitched a shutout for the White Sox and got the hen.

A LEFT FIELDER named Ken Williams and a catcher named Pat Collins, acting somewhat in unison as members of the St. Louis Browns, achieved a sort of immortality one afternoon in the late 1920s. From a standing start, Ken and Pat succeeded in making five wild throws all within the space of about one minute.

The Browns were playing Cleveland, and the Indians had three men on base. The next Cleveland batter hit an easy fly to left—the blow that inaugurated all the goofiness. Williams caught the ball and r'ared back to throw to the plate in an attempt to nip the runner who had tagged up and then started for home. The throw was wild, arriving far off to one side of the plate. Catcher Collins, however, stopped it and, realizing there was no chance to catch the man at home, threw toward third in the hope of getting the runner coming down from second. This throw was vagrant and passed a dozen feet over the third baseman's head. Left-fielder Williams got it again, and again heaved it toward the plate. His second throw was worse than his first but Collins at least stopped it. By this time the runner who had been on second was rounding second and heading for third, so once again Collins drew a bead on the third baseman and let go, and his throw came closer to the shortstop than it did to third.

Now for the third time Williams in left saw the ball coming into his precinct. The score in wild throws, at this point, stood two for Williams and two for Collins, and Williams was after the title, apparently. A third Cleveland runner was now heading for home, so Williams let loose a magnificent wild throw. This one didn't even come close to home plate, but flew straight into the Browns' dugout. That, technically, ended the sequence of wild throws. In the dugout Jimmy Austin, one of the St. Louis coaches, picked the ball up in a gingerly manner and dropped it into a bucket of water. "That ball," he remarked, "is too hot for our boys to handle."

JIMMY O'CONNOR, outfielder with Roanoke in the Piedmont League, came to bat in the eighth inning of a game against Lynchburg with three men on base and two out. Jimmy was a weak hitter, batting just a trifle above .200, and nobody expected anything spectacular from him in this situation.

Charlie Maxwell was the Roanoke runner on third, and as the first pitch was delivered, Charlie started down the line. Jimmy swung at the ball, bouncing it down the third-base line. With two men out it looked like a cinch play at first and the third baseman pegged the ball across the diamond. It went into the dirt, however, and Jimmy was safe. Yet no run scored.

When Jimmy hit that ball, his bat broke in half. The fat end flew down the third-base line, where it met up with Maxwell as he was charging in to the plate. It hit Maxwell a cracking blow on the knee and down he went in a heap. He couldn't get up, and none of the runners could pass him to score. So the first baseman simply threw the ball to the catcher, and the catcher walked out and tagged the fallen runner for the third out, and that was that.

BILL WERBER, who did a lot of major-league in-
fielding in his time, is today a prosperous insurance
man. There is evidence that Bill had a natural affin-
ity for the insurance game long before he left baseball.

He was with the Cincinnati Reds on a day when they played
the Giants. During the game one of the Giant outfielders mis-
judged a fly ball and, in so doing, crashed to the ground in an
ungainly heap.

That evening the clumsy Giant asked at the hotel desk for
his mail. The clerk handed him an envelope with his name on
it. He opened it and read:

"See Bill Werber for Accident Insurance. You surely need it,
judging by the way you handle yourself in the field."

THE CLOVIS TEAM of the West Texas-New
Mexico League was having a rough time of it midway in the season of 1940. The team was losing
twice as many games as it won and was occupying the cellar.
Manager Howard Taylor said over and over that something
downright radical had to be done. He didn't know quite what.

The players themselves were agreed that a large jinx was
hanging over them—some dirty, low-down inanimate object
was putting the whammy on them for fair. They tried to find
out what it was. One particular player, who was inclined to be
rather psychic about such matters, said he thought it was the

bats—that the team's bats ought to be destroyed. Manager Taylor refused, contending that his men would look slightly ridiculous up there swinging with barrel staves or brooms. Then up spoke an infielder:

"Hell, fellas," he said, "I know the answer. Clem's got pretty close to the answer. It's not the bats—it's that dern bat box."

Why, certainly. That dern bat box was the villain. Clear as anything on earth. So they pulled out all the bats and toted the box out to the pitcher's mound and burned it there. In less than a month the team had achieved such winning ways that it ranked fifth in the standings.

PEOPLE in Johnstown, Pennsylvania, are understandably sensitive about water. They still drink it, and wash in it, but they don't like to have it coming at them in sudden rushes. Several years ago a policeman, walking his beat in the downtown section of Johnstown, got a sudden rush of water. It was in a paper bag that had been dropped out of a window in a hotel, and it struck the copper on the head.

He was a policeman with the mind of a detective. He knew that when paper bags full of water come out of hotel windows, the chances are that ballplayers are involved. It is and has been for many years a favorite evening pastime of traveling ballplayers.

The policeman, mad as a wet cop, stomped into the hotel and asked if there were any ballplayers in the house. Yes, there was a team stopping in the place. A quick check revealed that only three members of the team were in their rooms. The policeman went upstairs and in five minutes had his man—a ballplayer named Joe Something who, on the following morning, paid a fifteen-dollar fine for flooding a Johnstown cop.

IT SOUNDS a little too pat, but an ancient sports writer says it really happened. A new pitcher was brought up to Brooklyn in the time of Wilbert Robinson. The young man was a happy and carefree sort of lad, and Uncle Robbie figured he didn't have the proper serious attitude toward baseball. However, he gave the boy his chance, sent him to the mound, and saw him pitch a good game until the eighth inning, when the enemy bats sent him to the showers.

The Dodgers lost the game and an unhappy Robbie trudged into the clubhouse, to be assaulted with song. Standing in front of the lockers, putting on his clothes, was the rookie pitcher, and he was singing at the top of his voice. The song he was singing was "Carry Me Back to Old Virginny."

Uncle Robbie walked up to him and said:

"Carry yourself back. You're on your way to the Virginia League tonight."

BIG BILL LANGE, famed outfielder for Chicago in the 1890s, was one of the sharpest ball hawks of his day. He was a remarkably fast man in everything but arithmetic. After a game in New York, Big Bill happened to bump into an old friend and the two adjourned to the bar for a session of beer drinking. Big Bill held the view that beer is palatable, and somehow he missed the train that carried his teammates on to Washington.

He did manage to get to Washington by game time the next day and, on arriving at the field, found Pop Anson, the Chicago manager, waiting for him. "You," said Anson, "are fined two hundred dollars. Now get out there and play some baseball."

Big Bill played spectacular ball all afternoon and in the ninth splintered a whole row of boards in the outfield fence, crashing up against it to catch a fly that saved the game for Chicago. As he limped in to the clubhouse, Manager Anson caught up with him. "Bill," said Pop, "that catch was worth two hundred dollars. You don't have to pay the fine."

Back at the Washington hotel, the outfielder retired to his

room, didn't come down for dinner, and everyone figured he was resting from the awful bruising he got in hitting that fence. At last Pop Anson sent another player up to check on Big Bill. The emissary returned shortly.

"He's settin' up there," he reported, "with a pencil and a lot of paper doin' a lot of cipherin'. He's tryin' to cipher out how many beers he can get for two hundred dollars."

LARRY DOYLE of the old New York Giants enjoys telling about the time he got the pinch walk. The Giants were locked in a close contest with Larry at bat, eager to get on base. The pitcher sent a fast ball down the inside, and Larry went into a Keystone Comedy pratfall in an effort to avoid being hit. Getting off the ground in a hurry, he trotted down toward first, slapping dust off his uniform. He knew the ball hadn't hit him, but he figured he might be able to run a bluff on Umpire Bill Klem.

He had almost reached first when he heard Klem yelling for him to come back. Larry turned and, as he started back toward the plate, he saw that John McGraw was storming out of the dugout. Klem's attention being diverted, Larry folded his arms as he walked slowly along the base path, and with his right hand began pinching the skin over his ribs. By the time he reached the plate he was ready to join McGraw in the argument.

"You say it didn't hit me!" he roared at Klem. "Well, looka this!" He yanked up his shirt and there on his side was a big red spot.

"Well, I'll be darned!" said Klem. "I'd a swore it didn't touch you. Go on—take your base."

235

THE MAJOR SYMPTOM of the period called The Era of Wonderful Nonsense was the endurance contest. All over the country people were trying to outdo one another in long-distance goofiness. Every flagpole had its sitter, and when the flagpoles ran out, the tree-sitters began their marathons. One man established a record for sitting humped up in a fireplace, while another assigned himself the job of reading the Bible aloud until he dropped. Young women stayed in swimming pools up to their necks until they turned navy blue, and certain young men had themselves buried alive. Baseball had to figure in this national lunacy somehow, and it did. In Bloomfield, New Jersey, eight ballplayers spent more than a hundred hours throwing baseballs from one to another around a circle. Somebody calculated that they averaged three thousand throws per hour.

THE REGISTRAR of Rutgers University went on a statistical excursion one day in 1929. His purpose was to determine the degree of intelligence, scholastically speaking, in each branch of sports. He concluded that athletes rank, in brightness, as follows:

1. Baseball players
2. Cross-country runners
3. Lacrosse players
4. Track runners and jumpers
5. Basketball players

6. Swimmers
7. Wrestlers
8. Football players

LIKELY it would be considered unethical today, but back in 1886 Pop Anson, the famous Chicago manager, "bought out" the Philadelphia club of the National League. The season was almost over, and Philadelphia was set to play a double-header with Detroit. If Philadelphia won both games, then Pop Anson's Chicago team would top Detroit and take the pennant.

So Anson announced that if the Philadelphia men beat Detroit in both games, he would buy a complete outfit of clothing and a trunk for each of fifteen players on the team.

Baseball salaries being what they were in those days, the Phillies went all out against Detroit, taking each of the two games by a one-run margin. The day after that the Philadelphia players all went shopping and before they were finished they had spent about $2,000 of Anson's money. He said he didn't mind at all—the pennant was worth every cent of it to him.

CERTAIN PITCHERS have been famous for periods in which they were wild beyond belief. During the time when Joe Krakauskas was pitching for the Washington Senators, a sports writer found himself converted into a war correspondent. He was in London during the bombing and one day he sat down while blockbusters were raining from the sky and wrote to a friend back home: "Actually I feel much safer than if I were sitting in the Washington ball park with Krakauskas on the mound."

One of the wildest pitches known to Gestalt psychology was thrown by Phil Marchildon, performing for the Athletics in a game at Detroit at 3:17 P.M., August 1, 1948.

Phil was erratic, to use a kindly expression, all through the game. In the ninth inning, for example, he walked two batters and hit a third, filling the bases, then walked the next man. It was in the fourth inning, however, that he demonstrated superior achievement in the matter of wildness. Phil leaned forward, squinting to get the sign, took dead aim on the catcher's mitt, and fired. Over in the grandstand, halfway between third base and the plate and ten rows back, a gentleman named Samuel Wexler, from Toledo, chose that moment to drop his scorecard. Mr. Wexler bent down to retrieve it. Boinnnng! Phil Marchildon's pitch hit him squarely on top of the head. It hurt but it wasn't serious, and Mr. Wexler was irritated for a while until someone pointed out that it was quite an honor to get hit on the head by perhaps the wildest pitch in all history.

AMONG all the superstitious notions held by ball-players down through the years, Jumping Joe Dugan's was certainly unique. Between innings and after rapid put-outs it is customary for the infielders to pepper the ball around the diamond, giving the appearance of exhilaration. It also is traditional on many clubs that the ball finally arrives in the glove of the third baseman and he tosses it to the pitcher for the resumption of play.

In the time he was playing third for the Yankees, Joe Dugan always insisted on switching the sequence of throws, for he believed that horrible luck would ensue if he was the infielder who eventually passed the ball on to the pitcher. He simply wouldn't do it, and required that one of the other infielders make the last toss.

One afternoon Joe's fellow infielders, Mark Koenig, Tony Lazzeri and Lou Gehrig, got together on a little scheme which they thought would *compel* Dugan to make the last throw to the pitcher. The signal was given just before the start of an inning. Waite Hoyt finished his warmup tosses and the catcher fired the ball down to Koenig at second. Koenig flipped it to Dugan and Dugan cocked his arm to shoot it across to Gehrig. He held his fire, however, because Lou was standing near first base, his back turned to Dugan, staring into the right-field stands. Jumping Joe now turned to throw to Koenig. Mark, too, had turned his back on the field; and so had Lazzeri. There was no place to throw the ball, except to the pitcher. On second thought, Dugan decided there *was* a place to throw it. He took dead aim and gave it all the strength he had, and the ball hit Koenig squarely in the butt.

In a sense, it was a moral victory for Dugan.

BEANS REARDON, the National League umpire, doesn't embarrass easily. There was an evening in the middle 1930s, however, when he sat in his St. Louis hotel room feeling thoroughly ashamed of himself. He was miserable in both mind and body, for the reason that during the afternoon, while umpiring a game between the Cubs and the Cardinals, he had been knocked out by the heat. There on the field, in front of everyone, Beans had begun to feel dizzy and faint, and then skyrockets and pinwheels started appearing before him, and he had withdrawn himself from action.

His embarrassment was acute because in his own mind he

figured the fans and the players were saying he "couldn't take it." Low in spirits, then, he sat in his room for a while and, hoping to get his thoughts away from his troubles, picked up a late edition of an afternoon newspaper. An item on page one caught his eye. It said that a camel, part of a circus showing in St. Louis, had been felled by the excessive heat that afternoon. What's more, the camel had died.

Mr. Reardon immediately began to feel better. What the hell, he said. If it had been hot enough to kill a camel—a creature fashioned by Nature to withstand the intense heat of the desert—then *he*, a mere Temperate Zone human, could be pardoned for getting a little dizzy. And Mr. Reardon worried no more.

JUDGE MARTIN FLEMING, presiding in Municipal Court at Chattanooga one summer day in 1932, listened to the damning testimony against a man named G. H. White. When all the facts were in Judge Fleming tilted back in his chair, gazed at the ceiling, and gave himself over to a few moments of juridical rumination.

The evidence was clear—this man White had, with malice aforethought, thrown a pop bottle at an umpire. The case was proved against him, and there he sat, pale and jittery, his guilt written all over him. Finally the judge spoke:

"Some of the decisions made by umpires would exasperate a saint. Some of our best citizens are outraged, and with good reason, by the treatment the Chattanooga baseball team has been receiving at the hands of the umpires. It is a wonder that these umpires are not deluged with soft-drink bottles. If they continue to operate on the local baseball diamond as they have in the past, we will soon have 'pop ball' instead of baseball. Case dismissed."

ONE SPRING DAY in 1946 the Brooklyn management hit upon an idea to boost attendance on Ladies' Day. Nylon hosiery was a post-pre-war scarcity, so the club announced that five hundred pairs would be given away to lady customers at the park on a certain afternoon. The offer brought 2,434 gals storming into Ebbets Field—most of whom didn't know and didn't care whether the Dodgers were playing the Cardinals or the River Bottom A. C. One journalistic observer reported that the five hundred females who got the nylons turned around and went home, and that a large proportion of the remaining 1,934, muttering in anger because they didn't get their hose, did likewise.

BURLEIGH GRIMES was one of the last of the spit-ball pitchers and it was a spitter that, late in his career, enabled him to make one of his more magnificent put-outs. He was on the mound for the Brooklyn Dodgers along toward the end of a tight game. The opposition got a man on third, with two out, and Old Burleigh grew just a trifle nervous. He had an intense urge to win this particular game, to demonstrate that he still had his stuff, and he had to prevent the batter from getting a hit. He knew that his spit ball was inclined to be somewhat erratic of late, but he knew that if he could deliver it with his old finesse, that batter wouldn't get a hit. So he threw a spitter. It didn't go where he intended it to go. The ball broke sharply downward as the base runner took a long lead. The pitch struck the edge of the plate and bounded

high in the air, arching back toward Burleigh. The runner decided this was it, and charged down the line. Burleigh himself came tearing off the mound, grabbed the ball as it came down, and kept on running. Pitcher and base runner arrived at the plate at approximately the same moment. A yard and a half of earth left the ground in the form of dust, and through the clouds could be seen arms and legs flailing wildly, and then one arm making a familiar gesture—the arm of the umpire calling the runner out. Burleigh's spitter was still an effective pitch.

AT LEAST ONCE in history a ball game was stalled on account of escaped convicts. A group of major-league players who wintered in California in

1941–42 got together as a team and went up to Folsom Prison to play a team of convicts. It was to be a thrilling day in the prison, and all of the inmates looked forward to it with eagerness—especially a couple of guys named Phil Gardner and Walt Mead. These two weren't interested in the ballplayers as ballplayers; the game was to be the instrument which would help them escape from Folsom.

The major-leaguers arrived at the prison and almost everybody was gathered at the playing field, and the game was just about to get started when the sirens began howling. Gardner and Mead were on their way.

Playing baseball was now out of the question, for the prisoners had to be locked up in order that all available guards could join in the chase. For once the bulk of the prison population was pulling for the guards, rather than the escaping men. They wanted to see those big shots play baseball, and damn those two bums for messin' up the detail.

Two and a half hours passed, and then came a whistle blast signifying that Gardner and Mead had been caught, and the umpire yelled "Play ball!" Gardner and Mead, alone among the convicts, didn't see the game—having indicated in advance that they had little interest in rounders.

MINOR-LEAGUE FANS apparently are more impressed by the procreative talents of their diamond heroes than are the fans in the majors. Kenny Sheehan, a pitcher for Oakland, took the mound against San Diego one afternoon in 1938. He was expecting a bundle from heaven at any moment and he was so excited that he began passing out cigars before the actual event. His fans couldn't wait, either. After Kenny had beaten San Diego, there was a ceremony at the plate, and a line of diapers was strung across the infield from third to first.

A similar shower was given Salty Parker, shortstop for Shreveport, later that same season. The day after Salty's daughter was born, the fans brought more than nine hundred packages of talcum powder, toys and baby clothes, plus three baby carriages and, by rough count, 3,977 diapers.

ED HEAD'S FATHER was mighty proud of him the day in 1938 when he pitched a no-hit game for a semipro team in Louisiana.

"Son," said the elder Head, "I'll give you an acre of land for every no-hit game you pitch as long as you play baseball."

Ed didn't think it was *too* liberal an offer, didn't feel that he'd ever become the state's leading landowner under such a deal. He explained to his father that he probably would never pitch another no-hitter even if his arm held out for a hundred years. Pop Head was reasonable, and heard the explanation, and then revised his offer: an acre for every shutout his son would pitch.

Ed went on to make quite a career for himself. He was with Abbeville in the Evangeline League, Montreal in the International, Brooklyn in the National, and St. Paul in the American Association. He kept books on his pitching record and when he finally hurt his arm and had to quit he had run his shutout total up to twenty-one, meaning he was the owner of twenty-one acres of good Louisiana land. Ed, incidentally, threw a no-hitter for the Dodgers against Boston in 1946, his last year in the majors. If his father's original offer had prevailed, he'd have been a two-acre man.

244

NO MATTER how strange a freak play may look to you on a ball field, don't jump to the conclusion that it never happened before. Dig back far enough and you'll probably find a parallel. Consider the occasion when Yogi Berra, catching for the Yankees, dealt with the opposition's try at a squeeze play. The batter laid down the bunt and the runner came charging in from third. Yogi snatched the ball from in front of the plate, tagged the bunter, tagged the runner coming down from third, and then tagged the umpire.

Turn back, now, to a game played thirty or forty years ago when a big man named Larry McLean was catching for Cincinnati. The pitcher threw wildly, with a runner on third. The ball got away from McLean. While he scampered after it, the runner came down from third and the pitcher raced in from the mound. When he got the ball, McLean didn't throw to the pitcher, but dashed back in time to tag the runner, then his own pitcher, and finally the umpire.

FIVE OR SIX YEARS AGO ballplayers in the North Carolina State League developed a sudden interest in market quotations on hay.

A grain-and-feed man named Harrington, in the town of Landis, offered a bale of hay to every player who hit a home run on the local grounds. When Mr. Harrington's attention was called to the fact that few modern ballplayers own horses, he put a rider on his offer: if a home-run hitter preferred the price of a bale instead of the hay, he could have it.

THEY HAD a "Brooklyn Against the World" celebration in Dodgertown on August 10, 1946, in connection with a sandlot championship series. Pronouncing the invocation was the Reverend John C. McCormack of St. James Pro-Cathedral. He prayed that the Brooklyn Dodgers would win the pennant and that Providence would see to it that he got tickets for the World Series.

A few minutes later Branch Rickey, boss of the Dodgers and himself an ordained minister, made his way to the box occupied by the priest and promised him the World Series tickets in the event the first part of the prayer was answered.

At that time Brooklyn had been in first place since May, but two weeks after the "Brooklyn Against the World" celebration, the Dodgers slipped into second place and finished the season there.

EVAR SWANSON, outfielder for the Cincinnati Reds, could never forget that disappearing ball hit by Norman McMillan of the Cubs one day in 1929 at Wrigley Field. It bewitched him, it bothered him, and it bewildered him.

Going into the eighth inning, the score was tied at 5 and 5. The Reds failed to score and then, in their half of the eighth, the Cubs loaded the bases. Out in the Cub bull pen, alongside the left-field foul line, Kenneth Penner began loosening up in case he was needed.

Norman McMillan came to bat and smashed a line drive just

inside third base. After passing the bag the ball headed into foul territory. Left-fielder Swanson had been playing McMillan over toward center, but now he came racing toward the foul line. He caught sight of the ball as it hit into an open gutter running along the base of the stands. Arriving on the spot, he looked frantically around but saw no ball. For a few moments Swanson played chicken-with-its-head-off, dashing madly this way and that. Meanwhile runs were pouring across the plate. The bewildered outfielder now saw Ken Penner's windbreaker lying on the ground in the bull pen. He pounced on it and shook it. Nothing came out. He glanced toward home plate and saw that the fourth run had scored, and so he gave up. He never did find that durn ball.

A short time later, however, Penner finished his warmup, walked over and picked up the jacket, started to thrust his right hand through the sleeve, and the hand encountered an object— the missing ball, to be sure.

IF YOU SPEND any time around Red Jones, who did a lot of capable umpiring in his time and who tells a lot of good stories, sooner or later you'll hear about the colored parson who doubled as umpire in an Alabama community.

Because the ballplayers had respect for their umpire's spiritual side, loud arguments were rare during their games and the language was usually quite sanitary. One day, however, a bad situation arose. Runners were on first and second with one out, and the preacher was umpiring behind the pitcher. The next batter hit a ground ball to short. The third baseman raced over to his bag, assuming the force play would be at third. The parson-umpire, on the same assumption, scampered toward third.

The shortstop, however, threw to second and the umpire had his back to the play. The action was ended when he did turn around, but he didn't hesitate on his decision. "Man's out!" he shouted. He was immediately surrounded by loudly angry ballplayers and this time they were using language that wasn't fit to eat. The clerical umpire raised both hands to command quiet, got it, and then announced firmly:

"Gent'men, I'm just a mortal, and mortals are weak and got to get guidance sometime. I rely on the Lord for guidance and I calls the plays the way He tells me. He told me the runner's out. Let us play ball!"

TEETH can be unpleasant things to have hanging around your jaws if you happen to be a ballplayer. Baseball record books, so scrupulously attentive to other details, ignore the fact that scores of players have had their teeth knocked out by baseballs. We have here a few little stories concerned with teeth and baseball. . . .

Lonny Frey, second baseman for the Cincinnati Reds, was in the throes of a horrible batting slump in May of 1943. Over a span of three weeks his average had dropped more than fifty points. In a game at the Polo Grounds a hard-thrown ball caught Lonny flush on the mouth, wrecking a number of teeth. He had to take a few days off for repairs, and when the dentist was all through with him and he returned to action, he began hitting the ball all over the premises, boosting his average by thirty points in fifteen days.

About ten years earlier a ballplayer named Joe Abreu, playing on the Pacific Coast, had some teeth loosened when a ground ball ignored his glove and struck him in the mouth. A girl spectator screamed with laughter and Joe, in great pain,

glared across the foul line in her direction, grumbling improper remarks. A day or so later he got a letter from her, apologizing for laughing at him, and he wrote back and said it was okay, and she wrote again, and they wound up by getting married.

More recently a shortstop named Melgaard, playing at Muncie, Indiana, got a special thrill when he larruped a long-distance triple. He was aware of the fact that a Muncie restaurant keeper had a standing offer of a nice prize to the local player who hit the longest drive in each game. In the final inning of this particular game a hot grounder came at Melgaard, took a bad hop, hit him in the mouth, and scattered his teeth. He was on his way to the dentist when he remembered his three-base hit, and the prize which he had won—an outsize tenderloin steak with all the trimmings. It is difficult to cuss with your teeth missing, but Melgaard managed it.

Victor Males of the Lancaster, Pennsylvania, club in the Inter-State League, joined the ranks of shortstops who have stopped bad hops with their teeth one afternoon in 1943. In the stands was a local dentist who had idolized ballplayers since boyhood. He sent word at once to Victor that if he'd come over to his office after the game, he'd repair all the damage for free.

When Charlie Grimm was managing the Cubs he was accustomed to taking his tooth problems to a dentist in Brooklyn. During a series between the Cubs and the Dodgers at Brooklyn, Charlie was having the dentist design and manufacture a new plate for him. After the Brooklyn series the Cubs moved over to the Polo Grounds. The work on the plate took longer than was anticipated. On the last day of the Giant series, when a double-header was on the bill, Charlie phoned the dentist and explained that he was departing for Philadelphia that evening and he had to have his store teeth. So the dentist hustled over to the Polo Grounds and between games of the double-header, finished off the job.

CHANCE by Steve Shilstone. A literary riddle, a baseball novel. 224 pages, $13 paperback, $20, hardcover. "A distillation of everything good having to do with the game of baseball. . . . Written with overwhelming passion." —*Minneapolis Star-Tribune*

THE PIGSKIN RABBI, by Willard Manus. 288 pages, hardcover, $23 ISBN: 1-891369-07-5 Comic, ribald novel about a young orthodox rabbi turned star quarterback of the Giants. Howlingly funny, and uplifting, too. "A vastly entertaining fable." —*San Francisco Chronicle*

TENNIS AND THE MEANING OF LIFE: A Literary Anthology of the Game. Edited by Jay Jennings. 336 pages, hardcover. ISBN: 1-55821-378-3 "It will be a delight—and perhaps a surprise—to those who know and care about literature." —*The New Yorker*

GOLF WITHOUT TEARS, by P. G. Wodehouse. The beloved humorist's short stories on golf and love. Paperback, 320 pages, $12.95, ISBN: 1-891369-08-3

THE ENCHANTED GOLF CLUBS, by Robert Marshall. Classic humorous golf novel. Paperback, 160 pages, $10.95 pb, ISBN: 1-891369-09-1

FULL COURT: Stories & Poems for Hoop Fans. Edited by Dennis Trudell. All the best fiction and poetry on basketball. 360 pages. ISBN: 1-55821-504-2 hardcover, $23; ISBN: 1-891369-12-1 paperback, $15. "Daring and revealing." —*Publishers Weekly*

HOCKEY SUR GLACE Stories by Peter LaSalle. 224 pages, hardcover, $20, ISBN: 1-55821-505-0. Paperback, $13, ISBN 1-891369-00-8. Hockey on ponds and rivers; hard times and strange characters. Enormous critical praise. "*Hockey Sur Glace* brims with affection for hockey—more accurately, for skating and winter." —*New York Times Book Review*

CAVEMAN POLITICS, by Jay Atkinson. A rugby novel and thriller. 304 pages, hardcover, $22. ISBN: 1-55821-565-4. "A transcendent metaphor for life." —*Publishers Weekly* "A wild ride through rugby's savage landscape." —*Tampa Times and Tribune*

METAL COWBOY: Tales from the Road Less Pedaled, by Joe Kurmaskie. 304 pages, hardcover, $23. ISBN: 1-891369-10-5. Funny, inspiring stories of traveling America by bicycle.

THE QUOTABLE CYCLIST: Great Moments of Bicycling Wisdom, Inspiration, and Humor. Edited by Bill Strickland. 360 pages, hardcover, $20. ISBN: 1-55821-563-8. A splendid collection of quotes, in a beautiful hardcover volume, with Keith Haring art.

NORTH WIND IN YOUR SPOKES: A novel of the Tour de France, by Hans Blickens-dorfer. 304 pages, hardcover, $23. ISBN: 1-891369-18-0

SPOKESONGS: Bicycle Travels on Three Continents, by Willie Weir. A wonderful travelogue, seeing the world by bike. 240 pages, hardcover, $21.00. ISBN: 1-891369-17-2

THE LITERARY CYCLIST: Great Bicycling Scenes in Literature Edited by James E. Starrs. 392 pages, paperback, $16.95. ISBN: 1-55821-562-X "A sparkling anthology." — *The Washington Post*

THE WHEELS OF CHANCE, by H. G. Wells. Classic cycling novel—funny, pastoral, and romantic—by renowned author. 284 pages, paperback, $12.95. ISBN: 1-55821-564-6

THE YELLOW JERSEY, by Ralph Hurne. 285 pages, paperback, $14.95. ISBN: 1-55821-452-6 "The greatest cycling novel ever written." —*Bicycling.*

THE WALKER'S LITERARY COMPANION, by Gilbert, Robinson, and Wallace. All the finest walks and hiking in literature. 400 pages, hardcover, $24. ISBN: 1-891369-19-9

THE RUNNER'S LITERARY COMPANION: Great Stories and Poems about Running. 336 pages, hardcover, $23. ISBN: 1-55821-335-X "A literary treasure trove." —*USA Today*

THE QUOTABLE RUNNER: Great Moments of Wisdom, Inspiration, Wrongheadedness and Humor. Edited by Mark Will-Weber. 304 pages, hardcover, $20. ISBN: 1-55821-420-8 "Keep this book close to you at all times. It can't help but improve your spirits and your running." —*Runner's World.*

THE ELEMENTS OF EFFORT: Reflections on the Art and Science of Running. By John Jerome. 240 pages, $20, hardcover. ISBN: 1-55821-614-6 Lucid, philosophical short essays. "Shows runners the deep structure of their passion." —*Runner's World*

FIRST MARATHONS: Personal Encounters with the 26.2-Mile Monster. Edited by Gail Kislevitz. Hardcover, 304 pages, $23, ISBN 1-55821-673-1. Paperback, $15, ISBN: 1-891369-11-3. "Inspiring reading." —*Wall Street Journal*.

THE OTHER KINGDOM, by Victor Price. Classic Irish running novel about a young miler. 220 pages, paperback, $14.95. ISBN: 1-55821-451-8 "An intriguing novel concerning the metaphysics of sport, and of excellence in general." —*The New York Times Book Review*

BONE GAMES: Extreme Sports, Shamanism, Zen, and the Search for Transcendence, by Rob Schultheis. 188 pages, paperback, $12.95. ISBN: 1-55821-506-9. A fascinating inquiry into visionary, spiritual, and preternatural experiences induced by ultra-endurance sports.

WIND, WAVES, AND SUNBURN: A Brief History of Marathon Swimming, by Conrad Wennerberg. 352 pages, paperback, $16.95. ISBN: 1-55821-615-4. "It should be in every coach's and swimmer's library." —*Swimming World*

THE QUOTABLE RUNNER TRAINING LOG. A practical version of the very popular book *The Quotable Runner*, featuring large inspirational quotes each week, and running trivia. Spiral-bound, $12.95, 192 pages. ISBN: 1-55821-613-8.

THE PENGUIN BRIGADE TRAINING LOG. *Runner's World* columnist John Bingham, hero to slow runners (penguins) everywhere, gives advice and exhortation in this useful training log. Spiral-bound, $12.95, 160 pages. ISBN: 1-55821-672-3.

THE SWEET SPOT IN TIME: The Search for Athletic Perfection, by John Jerome. 352 pages, paperback, $16. ISBN: 1-891369-01-6. A fascinating book on how athletes achieve their greatest moments. A must-read for all thinking athletes.

STAYING WITH IT: On Becoming an Athlete, by John Jerome. 240 pages, paperback, $14. ISBN: 1 -891369-02-4. The story of the author's quest for excellence as a masters swimmer. What he teaches about human physiology is applicable to all sports and ages.

STAYING SUPPLE: The Bountiful Pleasures of Stretching, by John Jerome. 160 pages, paperback, $13. ISBN: 1 -891369-03-2. An intelligent and very useful stretching book for all athletes.

THE ATHLETIC CLASSICS OF JOHN JEROME. Deluxe boxed gift set of the three above titles, with gold stamping on the case. $45. ISBN: 1-891369-04-0

TOWARD THE SUN: The Collected Sports Stories of Kent Nelson. 248 pages, hardcover, $20. ISBN: 1 -891369-05-9. Haunting, intense stories about the pain and beauty of life and sports.

EYE ON THE SEA: Reflections on the Boating Life, by Mary Jane Hayes. Poetic, insightful meditations on the joys of being afloat. 224 pages, hardcover, $22. ISBN: 1-891369-06-7 "Find this one and buy a few for gifts. It's a keeper." —*Northeast Sailing Life*

Dont's miss **PERFECT SILENCE**, by Jeff Hutton. One of the finest novels ever written—war, death, loss, love, redemption, and baseball. Publication date: September 2000.

BREAKAWAY BOOKS

IN BOOKSTORES EVERYWHERE

1-800-548-4348

Visit our website—**www.breakawaybooks.com**

FOL
APR 17 2024